LOW
RISK
RULES

A
WEALTH
PRESERVATION
MANIFESTO

GEOFF SAAB

LOW RISK RULES

PAGE TWO

Cataloguing in publication information is available from Library and Archives Canada.

ISBN 978-1-77458-174-2 (paperback)
ISBN 978-1-77458-175-9 (ebook)

Page Two
pagetwo.com

Edited by Amanda Lewis and James Harbeck
Copyedited by Melissa Edwards
Cover design by Cameron McKague
Interior design by Taysia Louie
Interior illustrations by Michelle Clement
Indexed by Donald Howes

geoffsaab.com

To the heroes who battle tirelessly,
to all those who support them,
and to my team: Effie, Daria, and Adriana.

CONTENTS

DISCLAIMER

WOULD LIKE to clarify something important before you start reading.

A lot of what you're about to read is made up.

Not the studies or facts cited—those are true.

I'm talking about any stories portrayed in this book that involve clients, friends, or other people I've met or had interactions with. All of these stories are fictional versions of actual events. The characters are composites. The details are usually fabricated. If you think you recognize someone you know in any of the stories included in this book, it's purely a coincidence.

Oh, and as the usual disclaimers go in books such as this that offer generalized thoughts on investment strategy: nothing in this book should be considered investment advice or a solicitation for business. These are my opinions only and do not reflect the views of anyone who employs me or associates with me on any professional (or non-professional!) basis. If you have a large portfolio to invest you should definitely hire someone smart and trustworthy to give you advice applicable to your own specific circumstances. There are many such people out there, you just need to know where to look. You might want to start with the awesome person who may have introduced you to this book!

INTRODUCTION

The end object of investment ought to be serenity.

GEORGE J.W. GOODMAN

NTREPRENEURS BREAK the rules. It's what got you to where you are today. But holding on to what you've earned demands different skills.

Pour yourself a drink. Grab a seat. Let's talk. I'm going to explain to you how the investment industry fails its clients, and what you can do to protect what you've worked so hard to build.

I've been working with wealthy clients on both sides of the table in various capacities for over a quarter century. I've been the accountant, the insurance guy, the financial planner, and the family office employee. Today, I'm the portfolio manager. I've experienced this industry from all angles—inside and out. And, frankly, I'm not crazy about what I've seen.

Helping someone manage their wealth is a tremendous responsibility. Because it's not just about what your money can buy—it's so much more. Once you know you have enough to comfortably retire, the responsibility increases in importance.

Because your wealth becomes about more than paying the bills. Now, it's about building a bridge from your present to your future. It's about possibility, opportunity, and freedom. It can also shape the legacy you leave when your earthly days are done. It demands wise stewardship.

And yet, many in the industry are less interested in understanding how they can help you, and more interested in the opportunity to sell you products that serve to turn your wealth into their income.

So while I'm writing directly to the entrepreneur—the rule breaker—this book outlines some rules you may actually want to follow.

It is a call to arms to empower you to take charge of your wealth, to create a life that is more meaningful to you, and to enrich the lives of your family and those around you.

It asks you to pursue a purpose-driven wealth management strategy that can create a legacy extending beyond your current needs and wants.

It makes the case against expensive, complex, and illiquid investments. And against an industry that pushes these products to unsuspecting clients.

It is a cry for rational and understandable investment strategies that support your confidence and conviction, increasing the odds of long-term success.

It is a celebration of equity investing, of owning pieces of successful businesses as a central element of wealth preservation and growth.

It will free your wealth from the shackles of the expensive and elaborate strategies too often pitched to the "high net worth" client.

My goal is to communicate a practical approach that resonates with entrepreneurs and business owners, simply and clearly.

Ultimately, *Low Risk Rules* is intended to call "high net worth" and "family office" investors back to basics. To turn away from expensive and illiquid investment products that enrich the companies selling them far more often than the investors themselves.

The end result of investing is a life lived with purpose, funded through wealth managed with intention. The material success afforded to you through your business isn't an ending—it is a beginning, and your liquid wealth exists to be in service to everything that is possible.

When your perspective changes—when you come to realize that your wealth exists to serve you—you will feel empowered to put your interests first. I call on entrepreneurs to fully own the fruits of their labor, and to not so easily hand it over to the salespeople.

I'm going to help you see through the fog and reveal a path to get you where you want to go. I hope to give you the clarity you need to ignore the noise and move forward with confidence.

I'm going to lay out an investment philosophy that, in my experience, resonates best with entrepreneurs.

Most importantly, I'm going to introduce an investment approach that generates superior returns over time. A lower-risk approach that will paradoxically earn you higher returns than gained by those who continue to invest as if they are still trying to get rich.

It's time to arm yourself with the truth about risk and return. To learn a new language and a new set of habits. Let's go!

1

SHIFT YOUR PERSPECTIVE

It would be some relief to our condition and our frailty if
all things were as slow in their perishing as they were
in their coming into being: but as it is, the growth of things
is a tardy process and their undoing is a rapid matter.

SENECA

This is water

Before we get started, I'm going to ask you to pause and consider your water.

In David Foster Wallace's now-famous 2005 commencement address to the graduating class at Kenyon College, he
tells the story of two fish swimming along. An older fish nods
at them as he passes and asks, "How's the water?" The two
young fish swim on for a bit, until one turns to the other and
asks, "What the hell is water?"

Everyone has their own "water." For the entrepreneur, a
state of elevated risk becomes second nature. A business
that is flying high one month could be barely scraping by the
next. Market conditions are ever-changing. Employees can be
fickle, but you feel an obligation to each and every family your

business supports. Even when you're at the top of your game, you know you could be knocked off tomorrow.

For so long, this was your life. The water you were immersed in.

When it comes to investing liquid wealth outside of your business, or after a sale, your perspective needs to change. The risk that was your partner in growing your wealth becomes an enemy in preserving it.

Because the skills required to build wealth are quite different from the skills required to protect wealth.

The instincts you have developed over the years may work against you when investing liquid wealth. It's time to learn a whole new set of skills, driven by a new perspective around what risk is and how it can work against you.

You must become aware of the water that you have been swimming in all these years, and the consequences it holds for your future.

Low Risk Rules is here to prepare you for the mindset shift that will help you successfully preserve the wealth you have worked so hard to build.

So ... how's the water?

The dark side of risk

Risk is an ever-present companion to the person who is pushing boundaries. Nothing great is accomplished without it.

Everyone who has started a business knows this. Everyone who has played a key role in building something valuable has risked something—whether it be their savings, borrowed money, or passing up the stability of a nine-to-five job.

Great success is not possible without risk.

And so you teach yourself to persist through adversity, to push on when the odds are against you, and to feel the fear and do it anyway. All essential elements to victory.

If we only pay attention to the success stories, we learn that risk pays off.

But for every successful business owner who mortgaged their home to get through a tough stretch, there are several others who borrowed and did not make it through to the other side.

If you repeated your life up to this point over a thousand times, how many of those simulations would have you positioned where you are today? In how many others would you have somehow failed, or been in a much less desirable spot?

The dark side of risk is the entrepreneur who took on too much debt, the investor who doubled down on a losing investment, or even the degenerate gambler who insisted that "one more hand" would turn their luck around.

But what's the alternative?

If we see facing down risk as virtuous and heroic, does it not follow that we see risk avoidance as undignified and cowardly?

Unfortunately, this is the impression many entrepreneurs bring with them to their investment portfolios. You have become habituated to the idea that taking risk is a necessary prerequisite to success. Or, even more dangerously, you see it as a key part of your identity.

Over the years, many of my entrepreneurial friends and clients have openly rebelled at the idea of cashing in some of their chips after a liquidity event. If you feel this way, you're not alone. It can almost seem like casting a vote of non-confidence against yourself.

But if you've been lucky enough to accumulate significant liquid wealth, and if your goal is now to preserve that wealth, the best way forward involves shifting your perspective. As the saying goes, there are old pilots, and there are bold pilots, but there are no old, bold pilots.

The instincts and habits you have developed over the years can sabotage your investment portfolio. Your attitude towards risk needs to change. You are going to shift from being a wealth *creator* to a wealth *protector*, and you must develop an awareness of the risk that you have immersed yourself in.

The temptation to keep gambling long after you've locked in a victory can cost you the security you've worked so hard to achieve. It seems far-fetched, but I've seen tremendous wealth vaporized by entrepreneurs who ignored the dark side of risk.

Time to concentrate on diversifying

There are many ways to build financial wealth. But a few ingredients are common among most who have built equity in a valuable business. A commitment to excellence. A vision for a better future. Customer focus. Hard work. Discipline. Persistence. Courage.

But think back, and along the way you'll likely recall a number of moments when things could have gone off the rails. Perhaps they did, and you were able to salvage it. But if we're honest, we know that luck plays a role in all of our successes. If a few things out of our control had gone differently along the way, we might not be sitting where we are today.

So building wealth is a consequence of hard work combined with a little luck. It takes humility to come to that realization, and, frankly, not everyone is able to accept it.

It's also a matter of concentration.

Concentration of effort—focusing on an ambitious goal to the exclusion of other activities.

And, importantly, concentration of your assets. Most business owners have the vast majority of their net worth tied up in their enterprise. This is how fortunes are made. Buffett in Berkshire Hathaway. Gates in Microsoft. Bezos in Amazon. Concentrating your investments can be a path to tremendous wealth.

We know intuitively that it wouldn't be prudent to build a portfolio out of a single public company's shares, but we don't think twice when we invest everything in a single private company that we run and control.

Here's the thing, though: whether it's your company or not, concentrating your wealth in a single asset is risky.

Imagine you had your entire wealth invested in shares of the Wang computer company instead of Microsoft. It sounds crazy today, but at its peak in the 1980s, Wang was generating $3 billion in annual revenue and employed over 33,000 people. Yes, people actually bought computers with "WANG" emblazoned on them in big, bold capital letters. But by 1992 the company was bankrupt and equity investors were wiped out.

If building wealth requires at least one successful, concentrated bet, protecting it requires the opposite. You need to protect yourself from tail risks. You need to diversify. This is about making sure that you benefit from growth in various parts of the economy over the long term, without trying to jump in and out. You just maintain exposure to them and ride the waves.

Diversification requires you to get comfortable with what is, by definition, mediocrity. A well-diversified portfolio is going to behave a lot like other well-diversified portfolios. This can be hard to accept if you've built your reputation and self-image on being exceptional. I'm not saying you can't build a portfolio that will perform exceptionally well over the long term. You can and should be trying to do that. But what I am saying is that you can't build a portfolio that will do that *all the time*, and attempting to do so is a mistake.

So when you're considering investing your liquid wealth outside of the business, or when you're investing after an exit, you need to pivot your perspective. The goal is no longer to build wealth. The goal is to build a moat around it in order to protect it. And you must adhere to different principles.

I've known several entrepreneurs who have leaped from startup to startup. They are not fulfilled without a constant challenge. Many of us know at least one individual who has left the stability of a successful company to join a new venture because they missed the excitement of starting something new.

If this is you, I encourage you to go for it, because the world needs more people like you. But with a caveat. You're no longer a beginner bootstrapping a startup. You've built resources that you can use to protect your future and that of your family. Set some of that wealth aside to build a conservative, diversified portfolio you can depend on in the future. Decide up front how much you want to risk in the new venture, and have contingency plans ready if your new ventures eventually need to raise more capital than you're willing to invest.

And then move forward with boldness and without fear, because we know that, no matter what happens, you've built that moat around your wealth. You've taken steps to safeguard the security you and your family may one day need. And that involves spreading out your bets.

So step one in protecting wealth is to reduce your risk by taking more, yet smaller, risks. Whether you like it or not, you're going to diversify.

2

FOCUS ON
YOUR NORTH STAR

For beyond the satisfaction of... necessities, all that the possession of wealth can achieve has a very small influence upon our happiness... indeed, wealth rather disturbs it, because the preservation of property entails a great many unavoidable anxieties.

ARTHUR SCHOPENHAUER

It begins with your purpose

Before we start down the road of *how* you're going to create your diversified investment portfolio, I want you to pause and think about your *why*.

There are infinite permutations of portfolios you can create for yourself. And a seemingly infinite number of very well-dressed advisors who are eager to help you out. But before we even go there, I want you to ponder the purpose this wealth can serve in your life.

What are we trying to do here?

I've had more than one client tell me over the years, "I want you to get me the highest return on my savings."

They say the customer is always right, but, with all humility, might I suggest that this is absolutely the wrong objective.

The only person who should be concerned with achieving the highest return on a portfolio is the one who is in a stock-picking contest. The way to win those is to take big, concentrated bets that either pay off huge or lose big. There's no room for hedging.

Anyone else, playing with real money, should be concerned with balancing risk and return. Because in order to shoot for the highest return, you have to be willing to lose it all. And for someone who is already wealthy and investing for security and wealth preservation, that simply doesn't make any sense. Remember... you only need to get rich once.

Portfolio management is ultimately about the delicate art of balancing the risk you're willing and able to take with the investment returns you need to achieve.

There's that risk word again. You can't separate it from your investment plan, because it's really the only factor under your control.

And so portfolio management is far more art than science, because despite the work that's been done to attempt to optimize the process, human emotions will interfere with the compounding of your capital. The risk you're willing to take will constantly be changing—with your own circumstances, but also with your perception of the economy, your confidence in your future, and the atmosphere of fear or greed surrounding you.

The goal of investing is *not*, therefore, to maximize returns. The returns you achieve are a byproduct of how the portfolio is constructed. And it should be constructed to serve you in a way that removes emotion from the decision-making process.

What are you trying to do?

If a young entrepreneur were to approach you, asking for funding or advice, the first thing you might do is ask to see their business plan. Many times along the way to building your own business you were likely asked for your own.

The business plan is a map that lays out where you are, where you're going, and how you're going to get there. It's a critically important document. Not because it's an accurate reflection of the future (it never is), but rather, because the process of creating it helps you envision the future, benchmark your progress, and lay out the key performance indicators that will lead you to success.

Entrepreneurs know this—they lived it.

So why, when it comes to managing their wealth outside of the business, do they neglect to impose the same discipline—either on themselves or on the people and organizations they entrust with their money?

Just as you had a business plan, you're going to want to have a wealth plan.

Your business plan was driven by a clear vision of where you wanted to be. The same goes for your wealth plan.

And how many of us have really, truly stopped to think about where we wanted our wealth to take us? The more you've been blessed with, the more important this becomes.

What can it do for us? For our families? For our communities?

Most people who go to see a financial planner have a pretty straightforward set of questions. When can we retire? Can we afford that vacation home? Should we be maxing out our retirement accounts or paying off our mortgage? But there are others who know they have more than enough to live the life they want to live, and I might argue that, in many respects, a wealth plan becomes much more challenging and important for these people.

You see, if you know you've got more than you need, complacency often sets in. Once that happens, you're less likely to critically evaluate investments. You won't care too much about the fees you're paying. You won't pursue tax planning opportunities. You'll spend more than you should, because why worry about keeping a budget?

The result is waste, and missed opportunity.

But someone who's got a vision and a purpose driving them will keep a closer watch over their wealth. Because they are thinking beyond their current needs, and have a greater purpose in mind. Every poor investment, every extra percentage point in fees, every dollar recklessly spent is a lost opportunity to benefit this greater cause.

Discovering your "why"

OK, but what should this greater cause be? What is your purpose?

There is no easy answer, and no one-size-fits-all way to discover it.

For some, it's as simple as the security and stress reduction of diversifying wealth outside of an operating business.

For others, it's about creating endowments to benefit future generations. Creating a legacy for your children, grandchildren, or community. Building a financial moat that will allow you to invest in a new business while ensuring your family's financial security.

The philanthropically inclined might consider setting up private foundations, or giving to existing charities. Money itself only goes so far—some entrepreneurs have chosen to partner with their favored charities—donating not just cash, but also management expertise.

The possibilities for identifying a greater purpose are really as wide as your imagination and your own unique passions and interests.

It could be contributing to infrastructure projects back home in the "old country."

It could be manifesting your love of art by creating a space for emerging artists to exhibit and sell their work.

It could be building a community of people around a shared hobby.

Or pursuing a dream that you otherwise would not have the financial wherewithal to support.

If you're reading this book, your purpose is not just about funding your retirement—you're likely well beyond that. The question is, what *else* can your wealth help you achieve? And how can it get you there?

If you have no idea where you want to go, don't feel lost or left behind. Most entrepreneurs have spent so much time singularly focused on their business that they really haven't given life outside of it a second thought. And they're very comfortable with trying, failing, and starting over, so that's what usually happens. It's a normal part of the process.

You won't have the answer on day one. And it will change and evolve over time. But beginning to think about it is a critical first step.

Always remember this one very important thing: your wealth exists to serve you and your family.

Work with a financial advisor who can ask the right questions to help you clarify your purpose—one who works to understand it as well as you do.

Realize that every dollar that you spend on fees or have trapped in underperforming investments is a dollar not devoted to this purpose.

Communicate it with your executors, children, and any other heirs so that decisions made in your estate reflect it.

Focus on it when deciding between options—buying or selling investments, spending on luxuries, or being asked to contribute to various philanthropic projects.

You got here by setting ambitious goals. Defying expectations. Being resourceful, creative, and making things happen. Let's apply that same focus to clarifying the purpose driving your goals for your liquid wealth.

Your "why" is going to evolve with you over the years. Keep your eyes on the horizon, but pay attention to the tailwinds. They will lead you where you belong.

Don't just think about what your money can buy you today. Your wealth represents a link between your present and your future. A connection between where you are today, and where you want to be tomorrow.

It's a tool you are going to use to build the bridge that will carry you to your next destination. And the one after that. And the one after that.

You might not know where you're going yet, but you have the opportunity to be ready for any potential road you may wish to travel.

Take care of what you have today, because you may not be given this opportunity again.

I want you to feel the responsibility, because it means that you will take it seriously. It is serious.

But I also want you to realize that the money itself is nothing more than a tool to achieve those dreams.

You're not there yet. The journey is only just beginning.

Freedom

When asked about your goals in pursuit of wealth, often the answer involves achievement of a certain level of freedom.

Many people choose entrepreneurship because they believe it gives them freedom. But those who build a business understand that this is largely an illusion. You don't have a boss expecting you to clock in from 9 to 5, but what you do have are customers whom you want to keep happy 24/7.

And so freedom takes a while to arrive. Eventually, with enough success, it's yours if you want it. Every business broker and investment banker will tell you that your goal as an entrepreneur is to build a business that can run without you.

As your business grows, and as your financial resources accumulate, you finally have the option to free yourself from constant customer demands and from doing the parts of the job you don't enjoy.

Liquid wealth gives you freedom of a different sort—financial freedom. Having wealth tied up in a business is tenuous. Even if things are wonderful today, tomorrow offers no guarantees. The business may encounter hard times or get disrupted. There may not be a buyer when it comes time to sell. And so there is a distinct difference between having wealth in a business and wealth in the form of cash and liquid assets.

Liquid wealth provides a level of freedom that you can't really replicate by owning a business, and this is what makes it so powerful. But with that freedom comes the potential for impulsive investing and spending, which makes it very easy to lose everything you've spent so long building up.

So, the liquidity brings with it a different kind of responsibility. Rather than being responsible for your employees, or the demands of your customers, you're responsible for yourself. Your future. Your family's security. Your legacy.

I'm not sure that these responsibilities are any less important than those associated with your business. In fact, I'd argue that they're more important. But if that's the case, why do so many entrepreneurs take them lightly? Why would you succumb to sales pitches, or invest in things you don't understand?

It's a totally different skill, but if entrepreneurs approached investing with the skepticism and street smarts they used in building their business, they'd be much better at it.

Think about your purpose, and build a portfolio that serves it. Focus on your North Star.

Money is a multiplier

Let me tell you about the very rich. They are the same as you and me.

With apologies to F. Scott Fitzgerald, over the years I have come to know this as true. Wealth doesn't eliminate problems. It just substitutes them with higher-class problems.

Being wealthy doesn't prevent you from worrying about money. It just changes the nature of your worries. Many of the newly wealthy feel they need to bury their insecurities under the false impression that, because they have money, they should have it all figured out. But I'm going to tell you that if you're insecure and confused when it comes to managing money, regardless of how much you have, it just means that you're human. I have never met anyone who did not carry that insecurity with them to some extent—wealthy or not.

Money doesn't change you. It makes you more of what you already are.

If you're generous, you will become more generous. Perhaps to a fault.

If you're frugal, you'll still be counting your pennies. You'll just have more of them to count.

If you're prone to obsess over money, your obsession may shift from worrying whether there's enough to worrying about how fast it's growing.

The problem is that too much money can give us the freedom to allow our less-constructive instincts to lead us down a dangerous path. I ask you to start with your purpose, because without a North Star your wealth can drag you places you didn't intend to go.

If you have an addictive personality, you may find yourself drifting deeper into gambling. Or alcohol. Or drugs.

If you're suspicious, you might think that everyone befriending you wants something.

If you're considering breaking rules, severing relationships, or taking a big personal risk, being "rich" might give you just the excuse you needed to go for it. Sometimes these decisions don't work out, and having cash in the bank won't comfort you if you've made a life-altering mistake.

Money is a multiplier.

It multiplies the good, and it multiplies the bad.

It demands self-awareness and solid relationships built on trust. It rewards patience. It punishes decisions made hastily.

Like a supercar with traction control turned off, it does not leave a margin for error if you hit the accelerator too hard.

And so you need to consider your goals, develop a plan, and implement a strategy to get you where you want to go. You've worked too hard to get to this point. It would be a shame to wreck your new Ferrari right after you drive it off the lot.

Eyes on the horizon

Paradoxically, the way to overcome the worst elements that wealth can introduce into your life is to *ignore the wealth*.

Don't focus on the money in the bank. Focus on what it can help you achieve.

If you've got a decent amount to retire on and a bit of a buffer, developing a plan is relatively simple. It's when you have more than you will need in your lifetime—*legacy wealth*—that things can get a bit more complicated. And the more you have, the harder this is.

Successfully managing legacy wealth is like walking a highwire.

Keep your eyes on your destination.

For God's sake, don't look down.

So when I say it begins with your purpose, I want you to focus on where you want to go.

First let's think about your parents, kids, grandchildren, and maybe even other family members or friends you'd like to help—today and in the future. Let's carve out current gifts and estate bequests, and know that the money will be there for them. Sounds easy enough, but don't forget that your future estate might be significantly larger than your current net worth. And so think carefully about how much you give to any single beneficiary. Just saying "my kids will split it" might give them far more than they are equipped to handle.

Remember Warren Buffett's sage advice: give your children enough "so that they would feel that they could do anything, but not so much that they could do nothing."

We also want to consider the impact we can have on our communities, and on causes that are meaningful to us. While making large donations in your estate is one way to give back, increasingly people want to witness firsthand the impact of their giving. There has also been a trend towards entrepreneurial donors becoming actively involved in the causes they support, lending their expertise and creativity in addition to financial support and thereby multiplying the effectiveness of their giving. You not only have extra money (and hopefully time!) on your hands, but also the skills and expertise to continue to make a difference in the world.

And this is where your horizons expand. Within abundance, you have the opportunity to find and create meaning. To actively shape your legacy.

By thinking about what you want this legacy to be, and focusing on how you can shape it, you can sidestep many of the troubles that liquid wealth can introduce.

But it's not enough to focus on your purpose—because liquid wealth is so different from illiquid wealth, it introduces behavioral issues that challenge the best of us.

3

YOU'RE BAD AT THIS

Know the enemy,
Know yourself,
And victory
Is never in doubt,
Not in a hundred battles.

SUN TZU

Your own worst enemy

Every entrepreneur worth their salt knows that competition is fierce, and that success requires an analysis of your strengths and weaknesses, as well as those of your competition, along the entire value chain.

It's clear that in business, the competition is your enemy.

But it takes a certain level of introspection to come to grips with the fact that, in investing, there is no external enemy. You're not in a competition with other traders, and the returns your annoying neighbor Frank brags about shouldn't matter one bit to you.

In investing, the enemy is *you*.

The enemy is your proclivity to do the wrong thing at the wrong time, and while being aware of behavioral pitfalls is helpful, it doesn't inoculate you from making those same mistakes. Because despite your best efforts, it's almost impossible to remove your emotions from the equation when you're investing your own money. There's simply no way around it.

And despite how successful you may have been in so many other parts of your life, odds are that you are bad at investing.

Please don't take it personally. So are almost all of us.

So much so that there's an entire field—behavioral finance—dedicated to researching and documenting all of the dumb things we do with our money.

The first step in addressing these various dumb things is to at least become aware of them. Now, that's not going to stop you from doing them, but at least you'll know what's causing your errors.

For example, I've lived my life entirely unsatisfied with two slices of pizza. I always want a third. Despite regretting it almost every time, I still reach for that third slice. I haven't learned. But at least I know my problem. Two pieces is not enough. Three is too much. And eating half a slice is a cop-out.

So before you reach for that proverbial third slice and have to deal with the inevitable consequences, I just want to open your eyes to a few key things investors consistently mess up.

We prefer complexity

In his book *What Works on Wall Street*, James O'Shaughnessy writes about an experiment conducted by psychosociologist Alex Bavelas. I'll summarize the experiment as briefly as I can and explain how it applies to our perception of finance and markets.

Two subjects—O'Shaughnessy calls them Smith and Jones—are given a task that neither has any expertise in. They are asked to distinguish between pictures of healthy and sick cells, using trial and error.

They can't see each other while the experiment takes place. In front of each of them are two buttons: one marked "healthy" and one marked "sick." The subjects are asked to select and press one button after they see each picture. After each guess, they are immediately informed via a signal light whether they guessed right or wrong.

Of the two participants, only Smith is getting true feedback. Jones is not getting feedback on his actual performance; rather, he is seeing the same feedback as Smith, which has nothing to do with his own answers.

After the first round of slides, a moderator asks both Smith and Jones to explain what they learned from the process—that is, what rules they have created in their minds to help them judge whether a cell is healthy or sick.

Smith's feedback is clear, direct, and simple. Almost too simple. Jones, on the other hand, has constructed an elaborate patchwork of concepts to explain the randomness he saw in his results.

Before the next round begins, both Smith and Jones are asked to predict who will score better in the next round. Both of them decide that Jones has a better grasp of choosing between sick and healthy cells. They have been fooled by the complex and elaborate explanations cooked up by Jones as a way to make sense of the random results. This was consistently observed with most of the Smiths and all of the Joneses.

Another study involving problem-solving experiments, published in April 2021 in *Nature*, found that "people consistently consider changes that add components over those that subtract them." In our weakness, we are instinctively attracted to solutions that are more complex. Elegance and simplicity do not come naturally to us at all.

When you think about how this applies to the financial markets, it makes perfect sense. The complex answer always seems more intelligent. We watch the financial news networks to hear experts explain the market's movements to us, and expect those same experts to predict which stocks will outperform tomorrow.

We look for patterns because we want to explain what happened and predict what we think will happen. And, just like Jones, if we look hard enough for a pattern, we'll be sure to find it!

The reality of most financial commentary is that we try to assign an explanation to market occurrences after the fact. We're Jones, getting random feedback on sick and healthy cells and trying hard to identify patterns. Or we're Smith, listening in awe to Jones's intelligent, thoughtful process, which we feel is superior to our own simple methods.

In any event, we need to be aware that we all have a bias towards complexity over simplicity, and this makes us vulnerable to mistakes: not just incorrect decisions, but also a preference for complex, illiquid, and costly investment products that may not actually provide any incremental benefit to us.

Understanding that our goal should be to pursue simplicity, not complexity, is an important step in designing a thoughtful investment strategy.

We discount luck

"The harder I work, the luckier I get." This quote is most commonly attributed to film producer Samuel Goldwyn. Then again, Thomas Jefferson is also quoted as saying, "I'm a great believer in luck, and I find the harder I work the more I have of it."

I don't know who was actually the first to say it, but the idea encapsulates the feelings of most people who have achieved great things.

It's true—what outsiders might perceive as luck has a way of presenting itself most often to the most well-prepared and hardest workers.

But one must be careful about discounting the role of randomness in our success.

The entrepreneur is prone to what psychologists call "self-attribution bias." This manifests itself in many ways—some harmful, some helpful.

We tend to ascribe our success to internal factors (I'm smart, I work hard, I'm a great problem solver) and our failures to external factors (the regulations were too restrictive, taxes made us uncompetitive, the weather did not cooperate).

Of course, this can be damaging if taken to an extreme, such as the belief that every bad outcome is someone else's fault. However, if harnessed in the right way, it can reinforce a belief in your own ability to improve your situation, which is unequivocally a good thing.

Individuals who see the world through this "internal locus of control" believe that their actions matter, and that they can control their environment and their circumstances. Outside forces, such as luck, are not a factor. They are the author of their own success.

And so it is with many entrepreneurs. Often, they meet the mere suggestion that they got lucky with hostility and derision. And I get it. The many hours of work. The sleepless nights. The dedication to fight through many struggles. It takes a certain type of hero to persevere through these challenges.

Indeed, studies have confirmed this theory. In a 2017 paper titled "Luck and Entrepreneurship," Liechti, Loderer, Peyer, and Waelchli study a survey of over 63,000 individuals to determine how different businesspeople think about luck. They find that "individuals who believe luck is important are reluctant to become entrepreneurs, and those that do exhibit lower commitment." This is not surprising. It confirms that when we talk about entrepreneurs, we're dealing with a group of people who don't believe much in luck.

But it's still important to acknowledge the role that factors outside of your control may have had on your success. Good timing. The mistakes of a competitor. Commodity prices. Currency exchange rates. The list goes on, and if we're honest with ourselves we can all identify factors that, had they been different, would have negatively impacted our success (or erased it altogether).

The thing about investing successfully is that you have to hand over much of your fate to luck. The right investment at the wrong time is just the wrong investment.

You must be confident in your analytical abilities, but not so confident that you can't admit when you're wrong. Where many entrepreneurs succeed through sheer will and determination, investors need to maintain a unique balance of confidence and humility.

A too-strong internal locus of control can kill an investor. No matter how solid your analysis is, you can't influence stock prices to move in the direction you want them to go through sheer force of will. The point of the game of investing is to tilt the odds ever so slightly in your favor. To maximize profits when you're right and minimize losses when you're wrong. It's a different state of mind from the one you might be used to. And it's why so many entrepreneurs have trouble adjusting to the investor's mindset.

We seek comfort in the familiar...

Businesspeople can have unique insider expertise in their respective industries, but this doesn't always translate to investment success. Although they might understand the nuances better than most, asset prices are often driven by other factors. This is where an understanding of business valuation comes in. It can take an outsider's view of an industry to truly understand whether the companies in it are fairly valued—not just relative to each other, but also to all of the other investments available around the world.

Your own section of the forest might be thriving and pleasant, but you are completely unaware that several miles away a fire has been sparked. Or that there's a more lush, more promising area over the next hill.

Worse, whether it's software or the oil patch, entrepreneurs often don't realize how much they are exposed to the fortunes of that single industry, and how little they are actually diversified.

I can build a pretty well-diversified portfolio of ten stocks, provided they are in different industries and have different geographic exposures. But if I buy ten medical device stocks, or ten wireless infrastructure companies, my diversification is an illusion.

Remember that a key reason for building a portfolio is to diversify your wealth, and so sticking close to home, whether that means industrial or geographic exposure, is often a mistake.

...and yet we crave novelty

The best stock portfolios tend to have very low turnover. "Lethargy bordering on sloth remains the cornerstone of our investment style," Warren Buffett wrote in his 1990 letter to shareholders.

Not only does low turnover make portfolios more tax efficient, it also means those portfolios were constructed with a long-term view of the companies owned, rather than with a view to buying stocks as a speculation for a quick flip.

Thanks to technology, buying a new stock has become akin to ordering something off Amazon. The desire can be generated by a whim (maybe you read something in the *Wall Street*

Journal this morning that inspired you to "invest" in another stock) and executed in seconds. It sends a rush of endorphins through your veins. You feel like you've done something productive. You've optimized your portfolio. You feel great about this decision.

But just like buying stuff online, by the time it arrives at your front door you might be wondering whether you really needed it. It might not be all it was cut out to be.

So here's the thing about the vast majority of financial news: you can (and should) ignore it.

Charlie Munger (Warren Buffett's right-hand man and one of the world's greatest thinkers) once said he has been reading *Barron's* for fifty years, and in all that time it has given him one investment idea. He said that idea led him to make $80 million "with almost no risk."

If you're like me, after reading a single issue of *Barron's* you might have at least a few new companies you're thinking of buying... or selling. And Charlie says that, in half a century, the publication has motivated him to make a grand total of *one* investment move.

We should all strive to be like Charlie.

Be an investment minimalist.

Don't buy that shit off Amazon.

And don't trade that stock because of some article you read.

Both wise decisions.

We are risk averse...

Entrepreneurs are no strangers to loss.

Cost overruns. Failed launches. Bad debts. Theft. The number of obstacles you've dealt with over the years are so many that you probably don't remember the majority of them. You don't let it faze you, though—because you can't.

But investing in liquid markets is different, primarily due to the immediacy of the feedback as prices fluctuate, and how it can lead us to constantly second-guess ourselves. Professional investors are well acquainted with prospect theory, from the famous 1979 Kahneman/Tversky study laying out all of the ways that humans behave irrationally in the face of uncertainty. This study forms the cornerstone of modern behavioral finance theory, and it says a lot about how we think about risk.

One of the main conclusions from this paper is that losses hurt more than gains feel good. For example, the average person would rather keep $100 they have in their pocket than risk it for a chance to have $250, even if it's a 50/50 proposition. In this case, the expected value of the wager is $125 and the rational response is always to take the bet, but most people don't, and you can attribute that to loss aversion.

When it comes to investing, this plays out in many ways.

I've had clients bring me a large sum—say, the proceeds from the sale of a business—and insist that the capital amount should never go below that number. This is a promise that is impossible to keep with any assurance.

It prevents us from taking smart and well-calculated risks for fear of losing money.

Loss aversion also causes investors to sell when they shouldn't.

It's a problem especially faced by investors who are new to public markets, and who are often spooked by volatility that proves to be temporary. I'm going to go into a lot more detail on this later on, because it can be a huge adjustment for entrepreneurs who are not used to seeing volatility in the day-to-day value of their assets.

... and yet we seek excitement

On the opposite side of the loss averse are those who pursue risk for a thrill. Entrepreneurs often find themselves unconsciously chasing risk out of boredom—especially after a business sale.

A gastronomic example is the Japanese fugu fish, which I learned about from *The Simpsons*.

I had to look it up. I was curious whether this fish—which, in the TV show, was supposedly improperly prepared and consumed by Homer, leaving him with only twenty-four hours to live—was an actual thing. Of course, truth is always stranger than fiction, and fugu is indeed a Japanese delicacy.

It turns out that this Japanese blowfish's organs contain tetrodotoxin, said to be 200 times more deadly than cyanide. The show's writers did take artistic license, though. In the show, an improperly sliced fugu would take twenty-four hours to kill Homer, but in real life it actually results in a much quicker death through systemic paralysis and loss of bodily functions (which would have made for a far less entertaining episode).

With an abundance of safe and delicious fish for diners to choose from, one would think that fugu would be thriving in their natural habitat, safe from the attention of sushi fanatics.

But you and I both know that's not the case, and it has everything to do with the irrational human need to pursue a thrill.

You can pay hundreds of dollars for a small portion of fugu. That's partly because the fish itself is rare and endangered. But it's also because only certain chefs are able to prepare it safely, and they must train for years to obtain the necessary certification to do so. The chef's final exam is to prepare and eat his own meal. How's that for a professional with skin in the game!

So if you're ordering fugu, you're paying a lot of money for a tiny portion, with a nonzero chance that you will die promptly and unpleasantly. Why do people do it? For many reasons. The rush. Bragging rights. Exclusivity. Some say that the tiny remnants of poison that still cling to the flesh produces a unique tingling on the lips. I'll just take their word for it.

No person thinking in strictly rational terms would order this meal, or attempt to eat it. But there's an innate human instinct to pursue the thrill. Some of us eat fugu. Some of us skydive. Some of us bet it all on the spin of a roulette wheel. And some of us take tremendous risks with investment capital, even when we know it's not the "smart" thing to do.

If you can't avoid the seductive call of the fugu, or the high-risk investment, at least make sure you understand the psychological drive that is attracting you to it, and don't confuse it with a more prudent approach. You can eat fugu once in your life to say you did it . . . but making it a staple in your diet might be tempting fate.

How to reconcile this innate desire to pursue a thrill with loss aversion? In the investing world it's an especially dangerous combination. There is a psychological urge to buy something only because it's going up, or to roll the dice on a lottery-type investment. Often this means you're buying high and hoping to sell higher. And then, when the price turns against you, loss aversion kicks in and leads you to sell low.

Entrepreneurs are used to taking risk, but not used to seeing their decisions "graded" by public markets so quickly, transparently, and irreversibly. If I try out a new product line or service offering, it might take a few months before I know whether or not it's a success, and I can course correct and tweak as we go based on feedback. But if I make a speculative investment, I might be immediately burned by a decline in value, where loss aversion kicks in and prompts me to sell for a loss.

If you're investing for a thrill, you're doing it wrong.

We follow the crowd

"I don't know how to be rich."

I've heard many variations of this phrase over the years, usually from people who have recently sold businesses and who are overwhelmed by the prospect of managing significant liquid wealth, and all the responsibilities that come with it.

There is a belief that there are things the newly wealthy are "supposed" to be doing, and so they often look to others to guide them. The right guidance in this situation can be very helpful. But, just as often, they end up repeating the same mistakes their friends and associates make.

I often see people with the same advisors as their friends, or who have invested in the same funds, or in the same private companies. Social proof is a powerful force. Many advisors have built their wealth management businesses around it. Bernie Madoff used it to bring in the cash needed to keep his pyramid scheme operating.

But the influence of social proof can be insidious, slowly causing you to adopt strategies that were designed for someone else. Additionally, wealthy investors sometimes come together in peer learning groups, and while these have some benefits they can also lead you down the wrong path. I'll cover this in a later section. For now, be aware that others may not have it figured out as well as they appear to. Be careful following the guidance of non-experts when it comes to managing your wealth.

We compare ourselves to others

One factor driving risk taking, or high portfolio turnover, or investment restlessness, is the fact that we are constantly comparing ourselves to others.

Studies show that most people would prefer to earn $80k while their neighbor earns $60k, rather than earn $100k when their neighbor earns $120k. This has a couple of insidious effects.

First of all, it's not healthy. No matter how much wealth you have, there will always be someone with more. Knowing that you have "enough" will allow you to live with a peace that a rich person always pursuing "more" will never know.

Second, this attitude is a large driver of bull markets and asset bubbles. As a stock market advance matures, you inevitably hear more stories about people you know getting rich. Often these people getting rich are absolute morons. And so you think, "If they can do it, it must be easy," and you open a brokerage account and start trading volatile and risky stuff just to try to catch up.

As Charles Kindleberger wrote in *Manias, Panics, and Crashes: A History of Financial Crises*, "There is nothing so disturbing to one's well-being and judgment as to see a friend get rich." It's a quote that cuts to the bone, only because it is so true.

Comparing ourselves to others is a flaw that encourages risk-taking at the wrong times. Because when everyone is making easy money and the market is ignoring risk, you need to be leaning in the other direction. As Buffett famously said, "Be fearful when others are greedy, and greedy when others are fearful."

What I'm asking you to do goes against human nature.

It requires self-awareness and self-control.

It's really difficult.

And that's why it works.

Whenever you think you've got it all figured out, remember . . . you're bad at this.

4

DON'T JUST
DO SOMETHING,
SIT THERE

---

*Men who can both be right and sit tight
are uncommon. I found it one of the hardest things
to learn. But it is only after [an investor] has
firmly grasped this that he can make big money.*
EDWIN LEFÈVRE

Your greatest challenge

After offering you a seemingly endless list of reasons why you
might be a bad investor, I'm saving the one that will likely be
your biggest challenge for last—in fact, I'm giving it its own
chapter. Of all of the mindset adjustments that the entrepreneur must make when managing their investment portfolio,
liquidity provides the largest temptation to misbehave. It's
the mechanism through which you can indulge so many of the
biases I've described so far, and take impulsive actions that
can cause permanent damage to your wealth.

Liquidity is the ability to quickly turn an asset into cash. As you can imagine, it can be quite an advantage to have the bulk of your wealth in liquid form.

It's also a leading cause of investment mistakes.

A private business is one of the most illiquid assets you can own. For better or worse, your investment in your business is a commitment you can't easily escape from.

But publicly traded equities (which of course are really just pieces of businesses) are one of the most liquid assets you can own.

These two assets are the exact same thing—an ownership interest in a business—but the element of liquidity is enough to make the ownership experience for each completely different.

In theory, liquidity is amazing. Wouldn't it be grand if you could sell your business in a matter of minutes without having to deal with investment bankers, or if you could sell your home without real estate agents?

However, in practice, liquidity allows us to act instantly on our worst impulses as investors.

There's an old saying in the investment world: everyone is a long-term investor until they start losing money. And the easier it is to sell, the more you will be tempted to do so.

In that sense, liquidity is like a loaded gun. It's extremely powerful and, at the right time, a potential lifesaver. But in the wrong hands at the wrong time it can cause irreparable harm.

Think of it like alcohol. Just the right amount can enhance an occasion. Too much can ruin it. And, just like we had to learn our drinking limits, even after we know what we're doing, even the best of us can occasionally slip into overindulgence and regret the consequences. If you're new to having control over significant liquid assets, you need to take the time to get to know your limits—don't head straight for the tequila.

Mr. Market in the mirror

Benjamin Graham, widely regarded as the father of modern value investing, explains the dangers of liquidity and the concept of value versus price through the story of Mr. Market, a character in his classic book, *The Intelligent Investor*. Imagine that Mr. Market is your business partner, and each day he offers to sell you his share of the business or buy your share of the business, at a different price. He tends to get over-emotional in reaction to the headlines of the day. And he's constantly throwing numbers at you that represent his estimate of the value of the business you operate together.

Of course, you know the business well and have confidence in your opinion of what it's worth. So on the days that Mr. Market is overly pessimistic, you should be buying his share of the business from him. On the days when he is extremely optimistic, you should be selling him your share. Graham presents Mr. Market as a character you can take advantage of, buying from him when prices are attractive and selling to him when they're overly optimistic.

In Graham's story, you are rational and levelheaded, while Mr. Market is wildly volatile and irrational... just like the actual market.

Now let's flip the story around. The danger that most fail to realize is that Mr. Market just might be *you!* No matter how stoic you think you are, in reality your emotions are subject to change based on all sorts of factors out of your own control, and you are likely to make poor decisions as a consequence. And so having the ability to buy and sell at will, with negligible transaction costs, ultimately can harm your long-term investment returns. When you're inundated with negative headlines and bad news, regardless of how rational you think you may be, you might just be tempted to sell your piece of a business for far less than the actual value.

We tend to operate in blissful ignorance of the value of our business, our home, or our real estate rental investments. You probably know a lot of people who have become wealthy by holding illiquid assets such as these over years and decades.

Imagine that on one bright, sunny day early in your business's evolution, Mr. Market comes into work in a radiant mood and offers to buy your share for double what you think it's worth. You just might accept that offer. But if the business grows over the coming years and decades, you would have been better off not selling to him at all. You might have gotten one over on him by selling him an asset worth $500k for $1M. But if the asset has grown over the years and is now worth $20M, who really won the trade? You may have won the battle on that particular day, but you lost the war.

And so even the parable of Mr. Market, revered by value investors for decades, leaves us susceptible to the temptations of liquidity and too focused on short-term price movements.

Let us not forget that in July 2006, a twenty-two-year-old Mark Zuckerberg refused an offer to sell Facebook to Yahoo for $1 billion. On that day, Mr. Market was wildly optimistic about the value of his business. But Zuckerberg knew that it had the potential to be worth far more.

Liquidity, by making it so easy to sell, can therefore cause us to make mistakes. Overtrading, or reacting to short-term market or economic news, is a surefire way of diminishing your total returns over time. Zuckerberg had temporary liquidity in his private company shares through the offer from Yahoo, and with his eyes firmly on the horizon, he refused to succumb to the billion-dollar temptation. Years later, his company achieved a market value of over one trillion dollars.

I'm not saying that holding on is always going to be the right decision, but if you have confidence in the long-term value of an asset, it's probably best to take advantage of Mr. Market's more pessimistic moods to buy more from him, while not being so quick to sell. And certainly don't fall victim to his pessimism and believe him when he tells you the business is losing value when you know better!

Most of the value of a business comes not from near-term earnings, but rather from what will be earned well into the distant future. If you understand this, you come to realize that the vast majority of business and financial news is short-term noise, and doesn't have any significant impact on the true value of a company's shares. It's easy to think past the headlines when you're making decisions about a business you control or an apartment building you intend to hold through thick and thin, but much harder when you can liquidate an investment in minutes, without getting up off the couch.

So while much of your net worth has now become more liquid than it was before, you'd be best served by continuing to think of it as illiquid. Just because you *can* buy and sell easily, doesn't mean you *should*. This is a bit like sticking to your diet when you know there's a box full of fresh pastries nearby... quite the challenge! It's actually easier if you're working with a professional money manager, and I'd argue that's a necessary element to investing wisely, especially if you are new to managing significant liquid wealth.

Whether your wealth is liquid or illiquid makes all the difference in the world. Remember the parable of Mr. Market. Don't let liquidity force errors in judgment.

Control your bias to action

Liquidity poses a variety of challenges for every investor. But the entrepreneur in particular has been conditioned in such a way that they are at the most risk.

In the early years of growing your business, you had to push forward despite what may have seemed like insurmountable odds working against you.

You had to seek out opportunities for growth. Almost as many experiments as you started were quickly jettisoned if they failed to show early promise.

There was no time for you to rest on your laurels. You can't put your rent payments on pause, and you need to make the next payroll in another two weeks. And again two weeks after that.

Success in business doesn't come from dreaming. It doesn't come from planning. It doesn't come from obsessing. It comes from executing.

The competition is an ever-present threat, looking to steal your market share. And it only gets more intense as time passes, because the more successful you are, the more they target you.

The life of a business is one of constant evolution, challenge, and change. You can't put it on pause, and you soon learn that inactivity will be penalized.

The famous Facebook corporate motto "Move Fast and Break Things" is a great philosophy if your goal is to foster innovation.

But it is the antithesis to intelligent investing.

Investors need to be patient. They have the luxury of waiting for the right opportunity, and then waiting for an investment thesis to play out. Overactivity in the form of excessive trading and chasing returns can be deadly.

The business world rewards pushing boundaries and experimentation, but investing often punishes it. The riskiest investments are often the most volatile, and so losses can be experienced swiftly. It's much harder to manage downside in a volatile investment than it is in your own business, because so much is out of your control, and emotions often get the best of you.

Warren Buffett has gone so far as to use the example of a punch card with only twenty investments you can make over your lifetime. Think very hard before committing your capital,

because you are punching your card. Although your investments might be liquid, you want to treat them as if they were
illiquid.

You have acclimated to the constant stress of life as an
entrepreneur, and you have a hard time imagining life any
other way. As an entrepreneur you often find that you need
an outlet for this nervous energy—particularly after a business
sale—because it has become a permanent part of your mindset. (I'll ask again ... how's the water?)

You're a natural-born bull, which is awesome. But while
you once roamed free, you now risk wreaking havoc in your
very own china shop.

So here's my suggestion: if you find yourself with enough
time to pay close attention to your portfolio, take up a challenging hobby that will stretch you—say, golf, painting, or
restoring classic cars. Anything. Just don't turn your investment portfolio into that outlet.

One of the keys to success in investing is to minimize the
number of decisions you have to make. The more decisions
you make, the greater the chance you will make a mistake.
And those mistakes can be costly.

Worse, overtrading is the enemy of compounding investment returns. You will buy and sell at the wrong time—there's
simply no way around it. Even the greatest investors in the
world do it.

Private investor Anthony Deden of Edelweiss Holdings
describes it this way: "The more frequently you look at something, the more frequently you second guess why you own it,
and what else you could own instead."

The more decisions we make, the greater the chance of
making a mistake.

This is compounded because we make poor decisions
under stress. Research shows that elevated cortisol levels
(an indication of biological stress) are associated with higher

portfolio turnover. The same elevated levels are associated with judgment errors and stress in social settings.

Essentially, the times when you might feel the need to buy and sell most are the precise times you shouldn't be doing those things.

It goes against everything you have learned during your time as an entrepreneur, but the fact is that in times of stress (like a market crash), the counterintuitive truth is that the best thing you can possibly do is nothing.

I have never once seen good come from a client obsessively tracking their portfolio, or suggesting stocks to buy or sell. Most investment managers will tell you that clients who try to influence portfolio decisions very reliably detract value. They want to sell when the news is at its bleakest. They want to buy into a sector when the financial news is broadcasting how much money everyone has made in it. Keep this rule in mind: by the time the news hits the front page, it's often too late to profit from it.

Overcoming your bias to action is perhaps the entrepreneur's biggest challenge when making decisions around their liquid wealth.

Gain mastery over liquidity. It can make it far too easy for you to do the wrong thing at exactly the wrong time.

5

YOU'RE GOOD AT THIS

---

*Wall Street is the only place that people
ride to in a Rolls-Royce to get
advice from people who take the subway.*

WARREN BUFFETT

You are an investor

Despite all of the behavioral reasons you might be bad at this investing thing, with the right frame of mind, most entrepreneurs should be good at it. Why? Because you've been investing for your whole life—that's how you built your business.

You never really considered what you were doing all these years to be investing. You just had your head down and were building a business. But every decision you made—to rent or lease property or machinery, for example, or to hire that superstar salesperson—was really an investment decision.

At its core, successful investing is allocating capital to its most efficient use. In plain English, this means that a dollar out needs to bring more dollars in. You had to work through this concept when you hired your first employee, invested in equipment, or decided to expand. Investing in a business whose shares trade on a stock exchange is no different from any other investment—you need to understand what kind of return to expect, and whether it makes sense to put your hard-earned capital at risk.

Running a business requires you to anticipate trends, and that's another key to investing. When there is little public interest, an investment idea is attractive and relatively cheap. But once it's on the front page or all the rage on social media, it might be too late to join the investing fray.

I don't have to explain to any successful entrepreneur how lonely it can sometimes feel to pursue a strategy you believe in but that others may think foolish. Again, this is something that is core to investing successfully. In the words of newsletter publisher James Grant, "Successful investing is having people agree with you . . . later."

Finally, you know the importance of assembling a strong team. This is a critical element of successful wealth management—ensuring that your investment manager, insurance advisor, accountant, and lawyer are all working together. You've done it before and you need to call these skills to the fore to ensure you have the right people helping you steer the ship through the seas to come. Technical skills matter, but more important is that they hold the right values and embrace the concept of teamwork.

Now that you're investing your liquid capital, you're going to need those skills more than ever.

There is certainly a distinction between a business operator and an investor, but if I told you that your success in business should make you a better investor than most of the "professionals" in the "investment industry," would you believe me? It's all about bringing the right lessons over, and leaving the wrong ones behind.

While you might expect the advisors and sales reps who come knocking to have some special expertise, they often have far less experience making investment decisions than you have. They might be really good at reciting return statistics and buzzwords handed to them by a marketing department, but chances are they haven't ever built a business and risked their own capital to do so. If you run a business, what you do every day is investing. What *they* do every day is sales.

Salespeople and marketing departments will often try to create an aura of mysticism around the investment process, making you believe that you can't do it without them. I implore you: when faced with investment industry jargon and sales pitches, don't forget the common-sense, street-smart values that got you here.

Once you have money, you are going to be pursued by financial advisors who will promise to give you access to "institutional quality" managers who can provide access to "non-correlated" assets such as private equity and hedge funds. You will be told that these "exclusive" opportunities are only available to the world's wealthiest "family offices" and that through their contacts and prestigious client list they can help you access these "world class" managers.

I'm going to let you in on a little secret: it's mostly bullshit.

The fact is, you know more about investing than a portfolio manager who went to an Ivy League school and who never put their own capital at risk to build something. Because, at its core, investing is about understanding businesses.

Don't let the sales guys intimidate you with numbers and charts. Those are either based on the past (with data they cherry-picked to make themselves look good) or on their own future projections (which are even more useless). If you hear talk about "alpha," "information ratio," or "tracking error," walk out the door and do not return.

Warren Buffett epitomizes this philosophy, and as he famously said, "I am a better investor because I am a business-man, and a better businessman because I am an investor."

Collecting businesses

I want you to think of your investment portfolio as a collection of businesses. It's that simple.

This is how we're going to construct a moat around your wealth. We're going to build a collection of businesses that we'll buy into at decent prices. We'll only buy a business if we can be reasonably sure that it will be bigger and more profitable three to five years from now—that if the stock market closed down for that time, we'd be happy to continue to own it. That's it.

Most entrepreneurs did not choose their industry with any significant premeditation. Often it's something they lucked into, or a niche they noticed needed filling, or something they inherited from a parent. When you started, you probably didn't analyze the industry's economic structure in any significant depth. You just got to work. Throughout the years you had to deal with all of the negative aspects of the business—whether it was cyclicality, capital intensity, labor relations—any number of things. You dealt with them because you had no choice.

Now you're building up your next empire, and you can choose the problems you want to deal with. You can pinpoint specific industries, companies within those industries, or management teams you respect. And in doing so, you can avoid all sorts of headaches and potential landmines. If you collect stakes in large, financially stable, dominant companies, a whole world of worries disappears.

Let's say you were designing the ideal business from scratch today—what are some of the characteristics you might want to see? To name just a few:

- A diversified supplier and customer base
- Selling a mission-critical product to a stable end market
- Low capital and financing needs

You can own a diversified basket of businesses that have those characteristics. It's quite amazing in that you can own perhaps the world's best asset for long-term growth—common stock—and at the same time have the benefit of full liquidity. You can generally sell most common stock positions within minutes while markets are open, and the only reason it would take that long is because you may not remember the password to your discount brokerage account.

It's a pretty remarkable process, when you stop to think about it. The investment industry really does take the stock market for granted when it tells you that investing in public stocks is too "boring" and convinces you to add complexity to your portfolio with more exclusive and exotic alternative investments.

Investing in the heroes

There are many ways to go about investing. One option is to hire a faceless group of suits to invest my money. They call it "allocating capital," and that sounds really intelligent. They will arrange and sort data to look for patterns, and then devise a trading strategy to exploit those opportunities as they present themselves. Over time, the returns accumulate, and the price chart looks like a jagged mountainside—up and to the right, with the occasional drop or notch on the way up. I get my report in the mail every quarter, open up the envelope, look at the chart and the dollar value, then tidily fold up the sheet and tuck it away in the folder with all of the other quarterly reports. And I move on with my life.

In order to "reduce risk" I will hire several of these faceless groups of suits. The mountain charts will look slightly different, but the overall pattern will be the same. I have a separate folder for each set of statements, and they live next to each other in my study desk drawer. I pull them out at tax time and send them to my accountant. And I move on with my life.

Occasionally, the numbers will drop and won't bounce back. One quarter, two quarters, now three... and the numbers don't seem to be coming up. The notch in the mountainside is getting larger and larger. All of a sudden I'm feeling less confident in this particular faceless group of suits, and I start seeking an alternative. If an ad catches my eye or a friend recommends a "great guy" he works with, I might consider switching. And the process starts anew. We pass this bump in the road, and I move on with my life.

This is one way to do it.

It becomes automatic and soulless. Like the morning coffee you chug every day on the way to work, sitting in traffic, preoccupied with the problems of the day ahead, the pick-up of the kids after school, and don't forget to swing by the dry cleaner on the way home. You drink the coffee by reflex, barely registering it as it passes your lips.

Do you remember the last time you really appreciated that morning cup of coffee? Because when you stop to really enjoy it, that morning cup is magic in a mug.

I'll admit I am a finance nerd, but hear me out on this one. Have you ever stopped to consider the magic of investing in a company's common shares?

You can *own* an actual piece of a company that you admire. This company may have been founded generations ago halfway around the world. But now you can own a small piece of it. You are effectively hiring that company's management to take care of the cash you invest with them.

Businesses aren't static entities. They are living things imbued with the spirit of their employees and leaders. They struggle. They adapt. They grow. They have cultures and personalities, which change over time. They stumble, and sometimes they fall. The proudest of them can decline and perish, and sometimes the ones left for dead miraculously rise from the ashes.

Being able to invest in a business is an amazing thing, and there is a soul and a spirit to doing it well and caring about it.

When you think about it that way, it changes everything. I'm not passively buying stocks as commodities. I'm buying pieces of businesses. I'm building my empire.

Perhaps the most important element to investment success is sticking with your plan through the inevitable downturns. Owning shares in companies with leadership teams you believe in is a phenomenal way to do that. You'll ride through highs and lows with them. If you made the right choices, you'll need to demonstrate patience and faith in their ability to weather the storms. The same management team you admire will use their ingenuity to solve problems and adapt as their environment changes. Think of your own business and how many times you faced an uncertain outlook. How many times you had to pivot your strategy in response to changing conditions. But you made it through.

If you think about it like this, you're not likely to be easily swayed in your opinion by the sensationalized clickbait headlines of the financial news sites, each linking to an article written by a reporter who has never run a business in their life.

The stock market is just a reflection of the business world you know so well. The faceless suits have it all wrong.

Did anyone expect Jeff Bezos to transform Amazon from an internet bookseller to a mammoth global retailer, an ubiquitous cloud software platform, a video and music service, and a grocery store?

Or Steve Jobs, resurrecting Apple from near death with the iPod and eventually revolutionizing modern computing with the iPhone?

Remember Hurricane Katrina, when Walmart's leadership and logistics proved more adept at getting supplies and provisions to New Orleans than the federal freaking government, with all of its unlimited resources?

These management teams can be your partners. They find a way to survive and prosper.

They are the heroes. Invest in *them*. Forget the suits!

When you buy a share of a corporation, you're recruiting their management team to manage your money for you. To find a way to prosper by maximizing long-term shareholder value. If they've proven their ability to do it in the past, you can have trust in them to continue to execute. Doesn't that sound better than hiring a faceless suit to shuffle your money around while optimizing equations littered with Greek letters?

It's not as complicated as the suits will have you believe.

The best investors are slowly building empires.

With a thoughtful approach and the right partners, you will find that you are actually pretty good at this.

6

LIVE SLOW, DIE OLD

People spend all this time trying to
figure out... "When should I invest?" And it's
such a waste of time. It's so futile.

PETER LYNCH

Don't outsmart yourself

The entrepreneurial life is often "live fast, die young."

When it comes to your savings, I'm going to ask you to "live slow, die old."

The best investors are slowly building empires. Accumulating quality businesses at good prices, letting earnings compound, and reinvesting cash flows. This is all there is to it. It will take time to get there. But you've got to start somewhere. So start small.

Investing profits slowly, over time, is a relatively straightforward process. But, for many entrepreneurs, money doesn't come out of the business in a steady stream. There are often very lean years followed by very profitable years. Sometimes there is the sale of a large asset, or an operating division.

Maybe an IPO. Or maybe a full sale of the business. And so you have to deal with investing lump sums, which can be challenging, because you will be tempted to try to time the market.

I can tell you one thing for sure—you don't want to sit in cash for too long. One thing I've heard from many individuals is that one of their biggest post-sale mistakes was sitting on cash, waiting for the perfect entry point, and watching the market rise without them.

If the market is going up, the longer you wait to move forward with an investment plan, the more you'll regret missing out on buying when stocks were "cheap," and end up sitting in cash indefinitely. Or worse, you'll capitulate and buy when prices are at their highest.

If the market is going down, you'll sit on your hands, waiting for the "all clear" to finally get invested, not realizing that when things look safest, prices are often at their highest. And so you wait . . . and wait . . . and watch prices rise while you sit in cash, wishing you had put a plan in place when you had a chance. And when the chance does come along, the news is too grim to act.

The entrepreneur knows that ideas without action are worthless. The same thing applies to investing. Don't hesitate your way to a "permanently temporary" cash portfolio.

You can manage this by ignoring the direction of the market while you're putting money to work. Don't obsess over your purchase price. Over the long term, decades from now, it won't matter whether you bought a few percentage points higher. Don't try to time it. You're very likely to outsmart yourself.

Take small steps . . . quickly

So, how quickly to invest?

Finance theory says that you invest it all on day one.

You see, academics have run the numbers over the past century-plus of stock market history, and this history tells us that, the vast majority of the time, you are better off investing everything immediately rather than trying to gradually increase market exposure.

I can't argue with that. It's true. The numbers say so. If I tell a client to invest everything right at the outset, I'll look like a genius the majority of the time.

But here lies one of the problems with relying too much on history.

Let's say you invest everything on the eve of the 1987 crash. Or the 2000 dotcom meltdown. Or the 2020 COVID crash.

History shows us that, each time, the market snaps back to new highs. But let me tell you something—living through these crashes is an entirely different feeling.

It's May of 2008. You just sold your business for net proceeds of $20 million, and you know that you now have enough money to safely see you through the rest of your life and to give your children a head start. You invest in a pretty standard portfolio—60 percent stocks, 40 percent bonds—and dream about your future. You can indulge in your racing hobby and already have your eye on the car you can see yourself taking onto the track next summer. You and your spouse are finally going to construct that wine cellar of your dreams and really build up that collection you started a few years ago. Your oldest is off to an Ivy League school next year, and you don't have to sweat over how you're going to pay for it. Things are taking shape. Life is good.

Fast forward to October of 2008. Lehman Brothers has collapsed. The world financial system is on the verge of a meltdown. And your portfolio is down 25 percent. In a few short months, your carefree future plans are put on ice and you have lost almost $5 million in the stock market. Almost a quarter of what you have spent the last twenty years of your life building has vanished into the ether.

Your financial advisor is telling you to stay the course. He's got a lot of fancy tables and charts showing that you made the right choice by investing everything up front.

It's cold comfort. You can't sleep at night. In a few months the stock market casino has cost you more wealth than your parents amassed in their entire working lives, a few times over.

You want to stop the pain. And so you sell. *I'll sell it all*, you think, *and buy back when things calm down*.

But you are shell-shocked. By the time you convince yourself that the economy is past the risk of a "double-dip" recession, it's 2013, and the market has more than doubled from where you decided to sell. So you wait for it to come back down before committing more cash. It never does.

Finance theory has failed you. It's great for textbooks and academic papers, and less helpful for guiding emotional, irrational humans in managing their life savings.

So my recommendation, counter to what the academic finance crew will likely tell you, is to scale in slowly over time.

I can't run any simulations and I can't point to any statistically significant evidence. But I can point to human nature, and to my experience dealing with clients who make the same mistakes over and over in volatile markets.

Investing too much, without appropriate experience in dealing with drawdowns, right before a significant market crash or pullback might just scare you enough to end your investment career.

So start off by committing a small amount to the market. Buy a bit more next month. And a bit more the month after.

Keep going. For how long? There's no definitive answer to this, and it depends on your comfort level with volatility. I would start with baby steps—maybe 5 to 10 percent of the total—and commit to slowly buying some stocks.

Keep it simple.

The companies you invest in should be solid blue chips with positive, steady earnings, preferably paying dividends.

The rest of your cash should go into bonds (or bank deposit notes), which are short term and safe—now is not the time to get cute trying to earn a high interest rate in some specialty product. The bonds are just there to get you some kind of return while you decide what comes next.

Sidestep the beginner mistakes

Now here are a few other things to avoid.

As I said, don't commit everything to the stock market on day one, particularly if you're not already experienced dealing with stock market volatility. Decide on a timetable to get fully invested and commit to it, but don't rush. If you ever start to feel nervous about your stock investments, dial it back.

Do not commit large chunks of your cash to illiquid investments. (I would classify this as anything you can't turn to cash within a week or so.) In my experience working with owners of newly liquid wealth, you are going to change your mind about your goals, perhaps multiple times, over the course of the next few years. Maintaining flexibility is critical.

Do not invest on the basis of a promised yield.

Here's what I mean by this. Many people get a lump-sum payout (let's say $10 million), decide how much they need each year to live comfortably (let's say $500k), and determine that as long as they earn a 5 percent yield on their portfolio, all is well.

Now, these days, a 5 percent yield is hard to get without assuming quite a bit of risk. But that doesn't stop many product pushers from creating portfolios that promise to return that 5 percent to you consistently, over time. Seems like a godsend! Here's the problem with many of these solutions.

First of all, if they're earning that yield on anything other than government bonds, the return of your original investment is not assured. Yes, I can create a portfolio that will yield a 5 percent annual dividend, but there's no guarantee that you'll see your original investment back. These days, I certainly can't do it in anything well diversified enough for you to call "safe."

Knowing this, many firms offer products that promise to yield you 5 percent each year, often by giving you your own money back. How does this work? Well, the portfolio might only earn income of 3 percent, but you'll get an extra 2 percent back each year as a "return of capital," which they will brag they can give to you "tax free." This isn't brilliant tax planning on their part—it's marketing. You actually aren't subject to tax when you take your own money back.

The risk with many of these solutions is that they tend to carry high fees, and over time require a 5 percent total return to pay you back. And if you've taken out that 5 percent each year, in good years and bad, on top of those higher-than-average fees, there's a very good chance you will find your principal balance depleted over time. The bottom line here is this: don't choose an advisor or an investment product on the basis of a promised yield. There is no magic solution to get you a magic number.

It may seem that I'm paradoxically encouraging you to both go fast and go slow. To get comfortable with risk, but also to avoid it. To prioritize safety, but not to believe the person who promises to protect you. And you might be wondering what on earth I'm talking about.

We're going to get there. For now, I want to encourage you to move forward, slowly. Stay liquid, and stay flexible. There are dangers along the path, and I'm going to give you the tools to avoid them.

7

YOUR ASSETS ARE
THEIR INCOME

---

*Wealthy people tend to have their preferences
dictated by a system meant to milk them.*

NASSIM NICHOLAS TALEB

The juice

If you don't know anything about sports betting, you might
assume that being a bookmaker is a 50/50 proposition. Someone places a bet, and you take the other side.

However, that's not quite how it works. In order to ensure
a profit and not leave themselves entirely at the mercy of the
New York Jets on a Monday night (God forbid!), bookmakers
actually earn money on a fee they call the vigorish (commonly
referred to as "vig" or "juice"). If a gambler wants to win $100,
they need to bet an extra 10 percent, or $110. The $10 juice is
there to tilt the odds in the bookmaker's favor over time.

The juice is generally a small amount. The cost of doing
business. But not enough to dissuade you from placing the bet.

The financial industry is basically built on the concept of the juice.

In the early days, mutual funds would take a chunk out of your initial investment—you gave them $100, and they put $95 to work in the market. This is juice! When people wised up to what was going on, the industry switched to "no-load" funds, which charged a flat (but much smaller) percentage fee every year. Different payment schedule. Same concept.

At every step, someone is squeezing a bit of juice out of your cash. Your advisor. The fund wholesaler. The fund company. The portfolio manager. All the way down the line. Someone's gotta pay for those golf sponsorships and sales conferences, after all.

Now, these guys are providing a service, and it's unfair to suggest that they're not adding value and earning their pay. But do you really need all those layers? How much more would you put in your pocket if not for all of the people earning a living off your portfolio?

Another problem that arises is that compensation is based on the assets that each advisor collects, not on the quality of their advice. And so what it takes to succeed in this business isn't competence or skill—it's sales ability. Specifically, wealth management professionals succeed by convincing very wealthy people that they should be the one they trust to manage their wealth. Regardless of whether they are actually qualified to do so.

So consider how much juice is being squeezed from your assets, and whether that juice is being well earned.

Buy relationships, not products

Finding the right person to work with isn't easy.

If you're in the market for "advice," being provided to you by an "advisor," then you're probably aware of the key problem preventing you from making a decision on who you should work with.

Advice is invisible. Without any detailed knowledge of wealth management or any of the functional areas that make up this industry (financial planning, investment management, insurance, and so on) how on earth are you supposed to evaluate the various people you're talking to?

Who is telling the truth about their skills? And how would you know?

The wealth management industry knows this and tries to make the quality of their service tangible in ways you can directly experience. It might be the mahogany wood and chocolate leather office decor. The heavy cotton stationery. The gold paper clips. The Italian suits and monogrammed French cuffs. The message is "we are successful and we work with a lot of successful people like you." In fact, Goldman Sachs in the 1970s actually included this as one of their "ten commandments" of business development: "Important people like to deal with other important people. Are you one?"

Unfortunately, these signals tell you nothing about the quality of the advice you're getting. Many times, they serve only to hide the fact that you're not getting very good advice at all. (It might also be a hint at where some of that juice might be going...)

So the first step in filtering through the smokescreen is to ignore it. Whether you're being pitched hot investment managers, clever tax plans, or elaborate insurance schemes, there is no shortage of salespeople making offers "you can't afford to miss out on."

Your first filter is going to be to immediately eliminate anyone who is more interested in selling you something than listening to what it is you're trying to accomplish. If you see any of the typical sales tactics (limited availability, time constraints, and so on), it's a huge red flag. You would think that these tricks are purely the purview of low-budget used car salesmen, but I've seen them used to pitch private equity funds and multi-million-dollar insurance strategies to people who would never fall for these same tricks in running their business.

Now, I don't have a problem with advisors who sell products to earn commissions, and I think it's important to stress that many of them are out there doing the right thing, despite some messed-up incentives. But as someone who gives financial advice for a living, what bothers me most about these pitches is that the vast majority of the time the salesperson makes zero effort to understand your situation and how the product might fit into it.

They are selling you a strategy they claim will help you win the game—without knowing what game you're playing.

The easy way to handle this, regardless of how attractive the offer seems, is to walk away.

The next mistake I see is advisors being selected on the basis of investment performance. It doesn't surprise me when the layperson thinks that the value added by a portfolio manager is their ability to predict markets. But it has often surprised me how many successful businesspeople think the same way.

Would you congratulate your purchasing manager for cutting costs only because the price of one your key inputs collapsed? Or would you punish a logistics manager for not having essential materials available if the plane those materials were on crashed en route to the distribution site?

We want to evaluate people based on factors that are within their control. Markets are not in anyone's control, and short-term price movements are most often entirely random.

The thing about investing is that separating the wisdom of a decision from the outcome is essential to understanding if the decision was a good one. And it's also incredibly difficult to do—even for professional investors.

Most of the time, short-term moves in a stock are determined by where the overall market is going. Think of stocks like boats floating in a bay—a rising tide will naturally lift all of them.

It's only over the long run that the wisdom of a given decision actually reveals itself. And when I talk about the long run, I'm talking years, not months. Too many people select an investment manager on the basis of prior performance, which may or may not be repeatable. In fact, studies show that it likely isn't.

It's important to keep in mind that you are not looking for products. You are not even looking for investment performance. You are looking to form a long-term relationship with a financial advisor built on trust. If it's purely transactional, you can be sure that they're going to disappear as soon as they collect their commission. If it's based only on investment returns, you'll be firing them as soon as their investment style falls out of favor (as all eventually do).

I've seen too many high-pressure sales tactics work in this industry, many victimizing people who should know better. When sitting across the table from a prospective advisor, you need to ask yourself: Do you trust this person? Do you understand what they're telling you? Are they listening to you?

Buy relationships, not products.

The HNW Industrial Complex

If you're reading this because you recently sold a business, you've probably been inundated with messages from financial advisors—both those inside your network, and those trying to find their way in. You might be feeling like a target, and that's because you are. You see, if you weren't already there before, you have entered the rarefied air of the High Net Worth client. The financial industry uses this term so much that we can just type "HNW" and everyone knows exactly what we're talking about.

You see, for financial advisors, it's often just as much work to bring on a small client as it is a larger one. And because most advisors earn money as a percentage of client assets, they of course want to focus on bringing on the clients who will give them the biggest bang for their buck.

And so was born the quest for the HNW client.

That's probably you.

Did you know you're a HNWI?

If you're really rich, you might even be UHNW!

For the uninitiated, that's "High Net Worth Individual," and the ultra-coveted "Ultra High Net Worth."

I've always hated these terms. Most obviously because this should be a business based on developing trusting relationships, and it's hard to trust someone who is targeting you only because of your plus-sized account.

But also because I've never had a client self-identify as "High Net Worth." Most would probably cringe at the suggestion. But we as an industry have decided to create a marketing machine around attracting these clients. Call it the High Net Worth Industrial Complex.

The industry is built on making the intangible tangible, and part of that is using language to convince you that you're being invited to partake in something special and exclusive.

The current hottest tag is a "family office." Lots of advisors talk about helping you manage "family wealth" and use terms like "generational" and "legacy" because it sounds really fancy and upscale!

By the time you're reading this book, there will likely be many other new angles through which the industry is pursuing wealthy clients.

In my experience, the more an advisor or firm uses these terms in their marketing, the less you should trust them.

Why your best interest doesn't matter

The HNW Industrial Complex does a great job of leaving out "inconvenient" information when it doesn't fit their sales narrative.

When you take your car into the mechanic, you've got your guard up. You don't know much about the inner workings of your engine, and you're not sure if the suggested repairs are necessary.

But there's something different about meeting with a financial advisor. From the suit and tie to the professional office space and thick, creamy stationery, there's a presumption of professionalism. It's the same feeling you get when meeting with your lawyer and accountant, and you trust *them*, right?

You will be presented with a lot of fancy charts (the jagged line always moving up and to the right!) and jargon that you don't quite understand but are too sheepish to ask about. So you start nodding along, and keep right on nodding as you are led through a sales process that ends with you signing on the dotted line and transferring your accounts over from XYZ Bank, who you feel never really appreciated your business, anyway.

But at any point in the process, did they mention the word "fiduciary"?

Let me put that another way. At any point in the process, did they mention that they are obligated to always act in your best interest?

If they didn't mention it, that just might be because they don't have to.

Does this make any sense to you? If not the client's, whose best interest are they operating in?

The majority of the investment industry operates under the "suitability" standard, meaning that while the investments or products must be "suitable" for you at the time they are sold to you, the advisor actually doesn't have to put your interests before their own.

So yes, the financial product you just bought may be suitable for you, in the same way that those skinny jeans actually do technically fit you. But your salesperson doesn't have to tell you that you look like a stuffed sausage in them.

It's crazy, but that's currently where we stand. You might think you're buying a timeless, elegant suit. But they're selling you skinny jeans.

Demand that your advisor be subject to the fiduciary standard. Every advisor will tell you that they feel a fiduciary responsibility to you, but far fewer are actually required to act this way at all times by law. Unfortunately, the rules are ever-changing, and vary by jurisdiction. At the moment, finding someone who is bound by fiduciary responsibility in the United States means finding an advisor who works at a Registered Investment Advisor firm (RIA). In Canada, it means seeking out an advisor registered as a portfolio manager.

It can get a bit messy, and so it's also advisable to seek someone who holds a Chartered Financial Analyst (CFA) designation—this professional accreditation demands that members operate at the highest ethical and professional standards in the investment industry. I can't emphasize enough how important this is. The costs could be huge if you work with someone who uses your life savings as a personal commission piggy bank.

Advice is invisible

Working with the wealthiest clients is seen as the pinnacle of the investment profession. Not only can it be more challenging and interesting, but, because fees are most often charged as a percentage of assets, it is also the most lucrative.

I don't begrudge anyone who is aiming for the top and trying to be the best. But here's the problem: the vast majority of investment advisors aren't qualified to work with wealthy clients with more complex needs. They simply don't have the technical skills or necessary experience. But they'll never tell you that, because too much is on the line. You don't let a large potential client walk out the door, no matter what it takes.

It's like going to see a physician who says he's qualified to operate on your brain tumor, even though he's a family doctor. It sounds ridiculous, but this happens in the financial industry all the time.

They will insist that they have all the experience you would want. They will brag about their planning expertise and experience working with extremely wealthy clients. You'll likely never know the truth.

Sadly, I've seen the consequences of this several times. It manifests itself in a number of ways: portfolios that are far too expensive, tax bills that are too high, planning opportunities that go unnoticed. And unless the client is fortunate enough to have someone wise enough to identify it or brave enough to point it out to them, they might never know.

The unfortunate truth is that you can get subpar advice for years—even decades—before you realize it. In the worst-case scenario, you'll never find out—but the executors of your estate certainly will.

Those who work with the wealthiest clients and pay them the attention they deserve know that it's not an easy path. It can be difficult to manage complex affairs, juggling tax, investments, businesses, and teams of professionals, often across multiple jurisdictions. It requires a personal touch and specialized expertise. And wealthy clients can be extraordinarily demanding. So the business doesn't necessarily scale well. If an advisor brags about working with a bunch of wealthy families, you might want to question whether they have the resources to add another to the mix.

Dealing with high-end clients also involves all sorts of unique complexities, and an honest advisor will likely be saying "I don't know" a lot. This isn't a weakness, it's a strength. An advisor who never says "I don't know" is not only likely very insecure about their ability to keep you as a client, they are also lying to you.

Lastly, don't choose your wealth manager based on glossy marketing. The best are usually too focused on serving clients to bother with it. One of the most knowledgeable advisors I've ever known did no marketing at all ... in fact, you would have been hard pressed to find out anything about him online. Grudgingly, he eventually put up a rudimentary website, which was nothing more than a home page with a mailing address and phone number. Now that takes confidence in his offering! It's a pattern I've noticed—some of the best advisors I've met and worked with have the worst marketing. So beware the extravagant brochure and polished sales pitch.

Remember: good advice is often indistinguishable from bad advice.

Advice is invisible.

8

CHALLENGE
THE PRESTIGE
INVESTMENT PITCH

---

*I know one guy . . . a very capable investor. I asked him,
"What returns do you tell your institutional clients you will earn
for them?" He said, "20 percent." I couldn't believe it, because
he knows that's impossible. But he said, "Charlie, if I gave them
a lower number, they wouldn't give me any money to invest!"*

CHARLIE MUNGER

The rules of the game

I was at my first cocktail hour of my first high-level private
wealth management conference when the rules of the game
were laid bare to me.

After a few brief stints in various sales jobs in the financial
industry, I was lucky enough to land a dream job in what today
is known as a "family office"—an organization dedicated
to serving a wealthy family in a bespoke and conflict-free

environment. To be honest, the whole concept of the family office was new to me, and the nascent industry was shrouded in mystery.

To build up my network, I decided to attend a conference that was advertised to wealthy families and their advisors. After arriving, I was a bit disillusioned to see that, among the hundreds of attendees, maybe only twenty-five were families or their staff. Instead, most of the people there were financial advisors and asset managers of various stripes, scouting for new clients.

It was the close of my first day there. I was severely under-dressed because I had forgotten the dress shirts that were hanging in my closet back home, and arriving late on a Sunday night meant that I had nowhere to buy clothes for the next day. The thing about being underdressed at an event like this is that it reveals that you are not a salesperson. So my jeans and untucked polo gave me away as a prime target in a sea of suits and ties.

I spent the majority of my day collecting business cards and feigning interest in silly hedge fund strategies I knew I'd never recommend to my clients. The cocktail reception was a welcome end to the day, with abundant hors d'oeuvres and generously poured cocktails. Those of us from families and family offices tried our best to congregate together in order to avoid having to listen to yet another sales pitch.

It was here that I made an acquaintance with an older fellow—let's call him Ted. Ted was an accountant by training—the chief financial officer of a long-forgotten company that had been sold for millions back in the 1970s. The company's owner wasn't sure what to do with his newfound liquid wealth, and so asked Ted to manage his investment portfolio and to run what eventually became his family office. Ted had been doing so for the past thirty years.

We shared an affinity for single malts, of which the bar was well stocked, and so Ted and I drank our fill and traded war stories. Gradually, as the thin veneer of professionalism fell away, courtesy of the Lagavulin, Ted leaned back, swigged what remained in his glass, and said, "It's all bullshit, isn't it?"

I squinted, as if asking what he was talking about.

"This whole farce," he said, waving his hand around the room. "It used to be easy. Like, really easy. In the '70s, there were a few really good hedge fund managers. We all knew who they were. It was pretty easy to get introduced to them, and they were usually able to sustain outperformance over time. The stock market was a lot less competitive, less efficient."

Although the hedge fund glory days he referred to were before my time, I nodded in agreement. I had always viewed "alternative" assets like hedge funds to be an unnecessary luxury that didn't really add much to portfolios. And so I naturally favored plain vanilla stocks and bonds for my clients. Not exciting, but a reliable and safe choice.

"These days," he sighed, "it's a crapshoot. Best to just throw it all in an index fund and call it a day."

I was taken aback by this. Just a few minutes earlier, Ted had been regaling me with details of the complex portfolio he had built for his client—over fifty funds, many employing special strategies, all in the name of earning some sort of elusive "uncorrelated excess return."

And so I asked him: "Why the elaborate portfolio then? Why don't you just buy the index?"

Ted smirked, leaned in, and lowered his voice. "Because then I'd be out of a job."

I laughed uncomfortably, but it wasn't a joke. "And you wouldn't be here right now," I said.

"Precisely." He tapped his temple with his index finger. "Let's order another round, kid. This is the good stuff."

Jedi mind tricks

Before I lay out an investment strategy that works, I want to warn you against some of the products that the HNW Industrial Complex is going to try to sell you. You see, Ted is a symptom of so much of what's wrong with the way things are done. And his clients are none the wiser.

Ted was ahead of the curve. He created a really diverse portfolio of complex investment funds, which over time has become the de facto standard among wealthy individuals and family offices.

Illiquid, meaning you can't access your cash quickly.

(All the better to capture that illiquidity premium, says Ted!)

High fees, which ultimately reduce your net returns.

(These exotic asset classes aren't cheap to invest in, and they require specialized expertise, says Ted!)

Ultra-diversified in a bunch of different funds, ultimately leaving the client owning a bit of everything.

(This is how we diversify our risk exposure, says Ted!)

The net result of that last strategy? No single investment can move the needle, and you essentially own an index fund. A very expensive index fund.

Mostly, Ted has built himself a very powerful moat: by constructing a complicated, inflexible, and over-diversified portfolio for his client, he has made sure that his job is secure. It's no wonder that this model has been replicated across the industry; worse, it's been marketed in such a way that has clients clamoring for these investments. It's a brilliant sales-Jedi mind trick that convinces otherwise shrewd businesspeople to ignore their best instincts.

The prestige investment problem

"I can get you into this really exclusive fund. They only accept money from big family offices and endowments. Harvard and Yale invest with them. I think the Rockefellers and Gates Foundation do as well. They don't take money from just anyone. This is a great opportunity."

Marketing techniques that appeal to your desire to invest in exclusive funds, or alongside well-known investors, are associated with investments that are expensive, illiquid, complex, and usually best avoided. I call these "prestige investments," and the "return" you can expect to earn from them is more about the psychic benefits of appealing to your ego than it is about the cash they will add to your portfolio. They are often an opening gambit that firms use to draw in wealthy prospective clients.

Let me tell you about a prestige portfolio that people were lining up to invest in. It was run by a guy you may have heard of... Bernie Madoff.

OK, that's not fair. Not all prestige investments are blatant pyramid schemes designed to separate you from your money. Most of them are simply elaborate, complicated funds with high fees designed to separate you from your money.

The perception of exclusivity is often illusory. But never doubt how profitable it can be—for the firm selling you these products.

This is where the HNW Industrial Complex manufacturing ramps up.

It's about selling clients what they want, not what they need. I've compared it to selling fast food. McDonald's didn't get to be the largest restaurant in the world by selling people salads.

Many firms that claim to specialize in the High Net Worth market offer a special suite of prestige investments aimed directly at the wealthy. It's an amazing tool for their salespeople because it not only attracts the HNW clients everyone is looking for, it also allows them to charge a premium to those clients.

As for these products, just like junk food, there's nothing wrong with the occasional treat, but making them the centerpiece of your diet is not a good idea. The problem with investment junk food is that, similar to actual junk food, you probably won't know that you've overdosed on it until it's too late.

These prestige funds take on many forms. But whether it's selling access to famous money managers or exotic strategies, the sales pitch usually includes the same elements. It's about seemingly "too good to be true" investments that are marketed as exclusive to the wealthiest clients. Far too often, the real benefits from these funds accrue not to the investor, but to the salesperson.

Let's face it, healthy food is a tough sell. I'm telling you to eat your vegetables, and there's an amazing BBQ place right across the street. You're listening to me, nodding along, understanding everything I'm saying ... but man, that brisket is calling you over.

From a marketing point of view, it's a lot easier to sell investment junk food. It's more exciting and more exclusive. There are also several benefits for the seller that they will conveniently leave out of the sales pitch.

It's time to arm you with that knowledge.

Illiquidity locks you in

Ted is as locked in as a financial advisor could be.

You're unlikely to fire him, because then you'll have to find someone else to oversee all of these different funds and managers. And you probably won't have any cause to fire him, because he owns so many funds and investments that he is virtually guaranteeing a very mediocre return. And that's just good enough for you to justify not going through the hassle and emotional upheaval of letting him go and changing course.

If you're being sold these funds through an external advisor, the products can often be proprietary to the advisor or firm selling them to you. So they're not portable if you decide to move on from the relationship. If you need to sell them before transferring your account out, you might be triggering tax. This could be enough to cause you to stay where you are.

Taxes aside, these investments are generally not marketable, meaning you can't necessarily sell them when you want to. Your investment can often be tied up for the better part of a decade, sometimes longer, which is a long time as far as economic cycles are concerned. Even if regular liquidity is offered, during market disruptions you'll often see a restriction on your ability to redeem that has been put in place in order to prevent the fund manager from having to sell illiquid assets into a crashing market—and this can be a disturbingly frequent occurrence. Frustratingly, this prevents you from getting your money out at the precise time you might want to reallocate to more attractive opportunities that may present themselves.

Put these factors together, and combine them with a portfolio that consists of several of these funds, all with staggered maturity dates, and you could be tied to a particular advisory firm for years.

The advantage to the advisor who got you into these funds is obvious. Not only did they suck you in with luxury branding touting exclusive investment access, but now the relationship (and more importantly, the annuity income associated with it) is also "sticky." You're not going anywhere—even if you want to.

Make no mistake, every investment manager's goal is to turn your assets into their annuity. One way to do this is to lock you into illiquid or proprietary investments and hope you don't notice. Inertia is a strong force in this business, and your desire to move on to a new firm must align with the exact moment that all of your funds are offering liquidity. If not, you could very well end up hanging around indefinitely, because transferring accounts is a hassle, and illiquidity makes it even more of a hassle.

Right off the bat, you can see the advantages that prestige investments offer the firms selling them to you. But there's more—in terms of both direct and indirect costs—that makes it an even worse deal for the investor.

9

COSTS MATTER

*To earn the highest of returns that
are realistically possible,
you should invest with simplicity.*

JOHN "JACK" BOGLE

Returns compound—and so do fees

One of the key themes of this book is that smart investing is actually quite simple. And this means that if someone is offering you an expensive fund (with base fees above 1 percent, or even worse, with a 15 or 20 percent performance fee tacked on), you're probably paying too much.

In a world where risk-free interest rates are pushing zero, it's really hard to justify an extra percent (or even half percent) in fees. This can compound over years and can easily cost you hundreds of thousands—or even millions—of dollars over time, depending on how much you're investing. Take the following chart as an example. You can see that an investor in the Ibbotson US large cap stock index has given up almost half of their gains since 1974 to fees at 1.5 percent.

IMPACT OF FEES ON INVESTMENT RETURNS

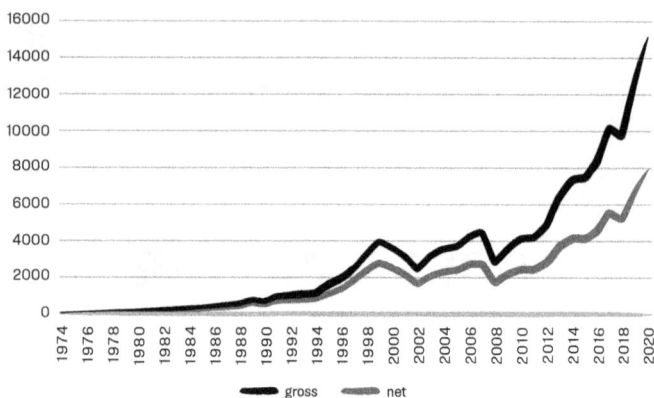

Data source: Morningstar Direct

You'd think this would be self-evident, but I'm consistently shocked at the very large portfolios I see where the client has no idea how much they are paying in annual fees. This adds up to serious money and can't be ignored.

So one of my first, most basic recommendations to anyone building a portfolio is to understand all of the fees you will be paying to invest. This includes not just what you're directly paying your advisor but also any fees embedded in the various funds they might be recommending. And this is where things can get really frustrating, because it is often very difficult to get a straight answer on how much you are paying all-in on such a portfolio. Your advisor definitely knows how much you're putting in his or her pocket but often doesn't keep track of exactly how much you're paying for the various products within the portfolio.

Now here's where I'm going to express an opinion that you need to take with a large grain of salt. I believe that if you're paying much more than 1 percent annually all-in on a large portfolio, you're paying too much. And the larger your portfolio is, the less it should be costing you, as a percentage of your total assets.

Having said that, there is a lot of nuance to understanding whether or not you're getting value for your fees. An advisor who charges over 1 percent and does zero planning work is not earning their fee, but someone else charging that same fee who is doing extensive financial and estate planning, and working with your accountant and lawyer, for example, might be a bargain in the long run.

But as far as portfolio construction goes, if the narrative you're being sold is that you're paying higher fees because of the exclusive prestige funds your advisor is magically able to get you access to, those higher fees are probably only going to subtract from the returns you keep in your pocket over time.

It doesn't matter how talented or insightful your manager is. At some point, if the fees are high enough, they can obliterate even the most impressive track record—as I'm about to show you.

The performance-fee parasite

Excessive fees are one of the most objectionable things about prestige investments. They almost always charge significantly more than plain vanilla investment strategies, thanks to complexity, specialized management, and extra costs associated with investing in exotic asset classes.

Worse, many prestige investments carry with them a much dreaded and despised fee structure that is a very efficient way of extracting juice. It's called the performance fee.

In a 2010 memo, UK-based investment manager Terry Smith laid bare the impact of the common "2 and 20" fee structure that many prestige funds use. If you're fortunate enough to not know what this is, it essentially means that the manager takes an annual fee of 2 percent of your assets plus a "performance fee" of 20 percent of the returns above a minimum specified hurdle rate.

Smith played out a "what-if" scenario with shocking results.

What if you invested a mere $1,000 with Warren Buffet through a purchase of shares of Berkshire Hathaway back in 1965?

By the end of 2009, your shares would have been worth $4.3 million.

But what if instead of investing alongside you in shares of Berkshire, Buffett had decided to set up a common hedge fund and get paid via the "2 and 20" convention?

Well, in that case, $4 million of the increase in value would have accrued to Buffett. You, the investor, whose capital was ultimately at risk, would have ended up with a mere $300,000.

This isn't just any manager. This is Warren Freaking Buffett. What's the likelihood that the manager in your "2 and 20" fund is going to come close to that long-term track record?

It's said that hedge funds are a compensation scheme masquerading as an asset class, and this is why. It's not about making money for investors—it's about making money managers rich by leveraging your capital.

Many will argue that the industry has responded to this by cutting fees, but as Smith wrote, "Two and twenty does not work. That does not mean that 1.5 percent and 15 percent is OK, or even 1 percent and 10 percent. Performance fees do not work."

Now, saying that the fees associated with prestige investments are too high isn't a terribly controversial position, and it's shared by many. But it gets worse. You will often find yourself paying even more to access these managers—fees on top of fees. And the reason for that is because investors seldom access prestige investments directly. They are generally offered through other advisors or through multi-family office type arrangements, and you're going to be paying them as well. Several levels of managers and advisors extracting their share of juice. Opacity and complicated performance fee structures make it very difficult to determine exactly what it's all costing you.

It's the HNW Industrial Complex at work.

In your business life you may have learned to pay up for quality work—the best professional advisors, the happiest employees, and the most motivated salespeople can all add more to the bottom line than they detract. But a professional investment manager isn't going to try harder or perform better because they're getting higher fees. It's a zero-sum game—every dollar you pay is one less dollar in your pocket and one less dollar to compound over time.

The more levels of people involved in managing your portfolio, the more it's going to cost you. Prestige investments are often the most blatant perpetrators of this entanglement against your investment returns. They are literal parasites, slowly eating away at your portfolio gains.

The costs of luxury

Investments sold as exclusive luxury products bring more than just financial costs. In all areas of your life, luxury also brings with it the burden of complexity.

It's counterintuitive, because luxury is sold to us as a way to reward ourselves. Whether it's an expensive Bordeaux or a high-end German car, the claim is that it makes your life more enjoyable. And, frankly, it's hard to argue with that. But these luxuries don't come without a cost—not just the obvious financial cost, but also the cost of more complexity introduced into your life.

I'll use the car as an example. You'll certainly benefit from the enhanced power, handling, braking ability, and technology while you're driving the car (and while it's under warranty). But with more features come more things that will potentially break or malfunction. You'll spend more time at the dealership. You'll worry more about what the next big repair might be. You'll enjoy the luxury, and you may justifiably believe it is worth the money you paid for it, but it will add complexity to your life.

Similarly, if you're a wine lover, your appreciation of grape varieties, vintages, and terroir has added depth and enjoyment to your life. But it's also added complexity—you will no longer be happy with a bottle of Two-Buck Chuck or the house wine served at your next banquet.

Still, in these areas, while luxury adds complexity, it can also serve to improve your enjoyment of life. What I have a hard time understanding is when people invite complexity into their lives with little to no added benefit. For me, what I own in my investment portfolio has absolutely no bearing on my happiness.

Prestige investments are sold as luxury products. If your advisor is branding themselves as a "family office" or touts "exclusive access" to star managers or brand-name funds, you are probably being sold a luxury product. This is all fine, as long as the performance created by these investments supports the higher prices you'll undoubtedly be paying. Spoiler alert … it usually does not.

Worse, these investments carry their own complexities. Before you heed the call of a highly diversified, "institutional quality" portfolio—of private equity or of hedge funds, along with everything that comes with these asset classes—understand what costs (both financial and mental) come with it, and ask yourself whether it's worth it.

To start, we've just seen that more complex strategies often come with higher fees and more complex fee structures (all the better to ensure you don't know exactly how much it's costing you), including performance fees. Performance fees are often sold as "aligning" the money manager's interest with your own, but, frankly, I don't need to claim 20 percent of my client's profits as my own in order to align my interests with theirs. (And if I do, I think that says something about me.) To paraphrase the great Jack Bogle, the unique thing about investing, unlike most things in life, is that you get what you *don't* pay for.

Research also becomes more difficult as complexity increases, and if you don't do it yourself, you have to hire someone to do it for you. Blindly handing money over to anyone, no matter how highly recommended they come, is a recipe for disaster. I hate to invoke the ghost of Bernie Madoff yet again, but there are several stories of individuals who didn't give him any money because they couldn't figure out how he generated his returns, or who was turned off by the lack of controls in place to safeguard assets. Due diligence is a necessary step that can save you from losing everything. Get ready to wade through endless offering memorandums and legal agreements they hope you'll never read.

Risk control and cash flow management can likewise become more difficult. For example, private equity funds don't require you to pay your entire commitment up front, but rather are funded over several years, as the manager identifies investment targets. In the meantime, you need to find a parking spot for the cash, and sacrifice longer-term returns for the benefit of remaining liquid and ready for "capital calls." Managing cash flows (both in and out) from this type of investment can be quite time consuming and occasionally challenging.

And don't forget the illiquidity that could lock you into unfavorable terms for years, and potentially prevent you from accessing your cash when you might need it.

I once knew someone who, by my rough estimate, had over twenty direct investments in private companies, about ten real estate rentals, and investments in about ten other limited partnerships, all in addition to a traditional investment portfolio. Oh, and on the side she was running a division of a multinational corporation.

These investments were hard to manage. Some had hung around on her books for decades, zombie companies barely hanging on. A couple were embroiled in various legal battles between founders, investors, and management. All together, they must have involved a collective several thousand pages of legal documents—shareholder and partnership agreements, rental contracts, and so on.

And after all was said and done, on average, she made the most money in a very simple portfolio of publicly traded stocks. Her lowest cost, lowest risk, and lowest maintenance investment was also her best performer. This same portfolio gave her the most control over her own fate (not being tied to a single firm), the most liquidity, and the most freedom. Oh, and the least headaches.

It's not sexy, nor does it feel exclusive. You won't be able to brag about it at your next cocktail party, and you're not going to travel to exotic locales for extravagant shareholder meetings. But it works.

I'm not saying you need to avoid alternative investments entirely, but I am saying that it's more work than you think. Legal paperwork, extra due diligence, and tax complexities are all part of the game. And if you're not doing it yourself (you won't want to—trust me), you're going to be paying someone else to do it for you. On top of all that, there's no guarantee of earning higher returns. And even if you do, less of those returns will make their way to your pocket because of all the extra costs.

In a way, what I'm talking about is investment minimalism. Complexity doesn't just cost money—it costs mindshare. It costs freedom. Expunge it from your investment portfolio, and see how much better you feel.

It will free space in your mind to focus on the things that really matter to you.

Imagine if your investment portfolio was actually one less thing you had to worry about.

10

YOU ARE NOT
AN INSTITUTION

---

*Simplicity has been difficult to implement in modern
life because it is against the spirit of a
certain brand of people who seek sophistication
so they can justify their profession.*

NASSIM NICHOLAS TALEB

The allocator model

We know that wealth preservation requires diversification, and
that means holding a wide variety of assets. But we also know
that we have an inherent preference for complexity, which can
so often lead us to make mistakes.

The question, then, is how much diversification is too much?
How do we balance the opposing forces at work—simplicity
that may not adequately diversify risk, versus complexity driving
up costs.

This is where we need to balance the sales pitches with a
good dose of prudence.

There are several basic ways you can go about building a portfolio.

1   You can buy stocks directly.

2   Or, if you decide you don't have the skill, time, or temperament to do it yourself, you can hire a portfolio manager to do it for you.

3   Or, if you decide that you'd prefer to spread your money
    around to different managers, you might end up with
    something that looks bit like this:

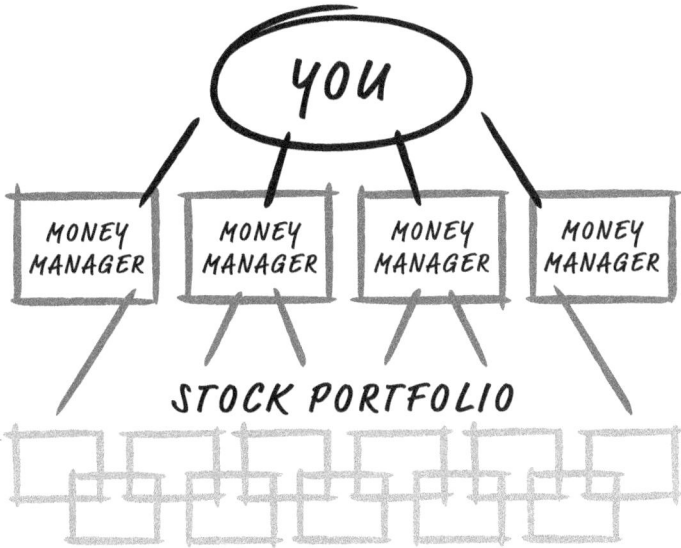

    Now things are starting to get a bit unwieldy. Depend-
ing on how many managers you've got, and what kinds of
different strategies they are employing, you may or may
not actually be well diversified. If they're all doing the
same basic thing, and owning the same basic stocks, you
might be better off with a single manager.

4   And so now there's some coordination required. You might
    find that you need someone on top to oversee the manag-
    ers. And now the portfolio looks like this:

YOU

MANAGER OF MANAGERS

| MONEY MANAGER | MONEY MANAGER | MONEY MANAGER | MONEY MANAGER | MONEY MANAGER |

STOCK PORTFOLIO

They go by many names—"managers of managers," "virtual chief investment officers," and too many more to name. But they all share one thing in common: none directly manage client assets. They all farm the job out to external managers.

For the sake of simplicity, let's call them "allocators." This is because they don't actually invest your money, but rather "allocate" it out to specialist managers who they hire to manage your funds on their behalf.

The model comes from the institutional investment world, where boards and investment committees are filled with professionals who volunteer to help an institution oversee money invested on behalf of its ultimate beneficiaries—a pension or endowment fund, for example.

These board members, while concerned with investment performance, are really more worried about getting sued by donors and/or beneficiaries.

And so they hire a professional consultant to guide their decisions. It's mostly a "Cover Your Ass" exercise. There is a theatrical element to these quarterly meetings. The consultant will explain the minutia of a particular manager's performance over the prior three-month period, and a boardroom full of executives will nod along. The consultant looks for reasons to replace a manager or put them "on watch," so as to give board members assurance that someone is closely monitoring the underperforming segments of the portfolio. The exercise repeats for each portfolio manager, and then repeats again each quarter.

Does the exercise actually contribute to investment returns? In a 2014 paper titled "Picking Winners? Investment Consultants' Recommendations of Fund Managers," Jenkinson, Jones, and Martinez conclude that they "find no evidence that these recommendations add value, suggesting that the search for winners, encouraged and guided by investment consultants, is fruitless."

So . . . there's that.

These boards tend to be full of successful individuals who also often happen to be wealthy, and so the industry began to offer the same model to wealthy families. The basic pitch is that they will help you hire the "best" managers in each asset class. And while it's dressed up in a veil of exclusivity, it's simply a close sibling to the stockbroker who builds you a portfolio of mutual funds.

They will recommend a bunch of different managers, diversifying among different styles. Let's have a growth manager, a value manager, a large-cap, a small-cap. Oh, and add a mid-cap, maybe an emerging markets specialist . . .

And on it goes. At the end of the day your portfolio has become so diversified that it becomes just another index fund—but with much higher fees.

The allocator problem

One obvious problem that should jump out at you is that the allocator model sure has a lot of layers of people between you and your money.

All of those people are getting paid.

That's a lot of juice.

Let's go back to basics on the HNW Industrial Complex. Imagine you own a profit-maximizing wealth management firm. You will have three financial goals:

* Charge as much as possible
* Retain the client for as long as possible
* Keep your own costs as low as possible

The allocator model facilitates all three at the same time. It's Ted's family office model, fully realized as a profitable wealth management business.

The allocators will make every effort to slice and dice your portfolio into tiny specialty sub-portfolios—based on strategy, company size, and geographic allocation. If you want to, you can oversee an empire of an infinite number of specialist managers, each of which in turn owns tens or even hundreds of individual securities. The allocators are no different from Ted: the complexity gives them a client for life—or at least creates a very sticky relationship. The beauty of this arrangement, for the allocator, is that there is minimal accountability. The allocator takes credit for getting you into well-performing funds, but the blame for underperformance always rests with the manager, not with the allocator who recommended them in the first place.

One reason some private clients and family offices prefer using allocators is because there's a perceived safety in numbers. Owning an ultra-diversified portfolio feeds the perception that choosing money managers is a lower-risk endeavor than buying stocks directly. And while it's true that it doesn't demand the same detailed analysis as investing directly in a company's shares, it does demand an entirely different type of analysis, which is perhaps more difficult.

Evaluating managers is tricky, even for professionals who do it for a living. Through my experience, I've come to believe it's more difficult than evaluating stocks. Inexperienced investors don't really have a chance. Why? Because while public companies are required to report all relevant and material information to investors, the most critical information about money managers is generally not public. Compounding the matter, there is no central "exchange" where you can see all of the managers and compare them against one another.

Even the allocators—the ones who will tell you they can choose "the best" managers for you—only deal with a tiny subset of the universe of managers. This is because many of the best managers choose not to play the allocator game, and so end up completely off the radar to the majority of investors.

It really requires a sixth sense to figure out if a manager has the magic you're looking for. And you have to meet hundreds of them over time to hone your ability to discriminate. If you are doing it yourself, or have a small staff, or—God forbid— someone working part time on this, the odds are stacked heavily against you. Inevitably you are going to end up investing with the managers who get in front of you first, or the ones your friends are already invested with. If you think these are likely to be "the best," you're fooling yourself.

There are a few factors that make choosing managers quite tricky.

The first is identifying the drivers of past returns, and separating luck from skill.

If a firm has a really impressive track record, you need to dig into the portfolio to understand what has driven that return. It is possible that one decision can drive a fund's outperformance over an extended period of time. I recall meeting with a manager who had a stellar record throughout the 1990s and into the early 2000s. This is an extraordinarily rare feat, as the managers who did well during the 1990s tech bubble are generally not the same ones who did well in the years after the crash, when value stocks led the market recovery.

When I asked the manager about their performance drivers, I didn't receive a satisfactory answer. And so I asked to take a close look at the portfolio. And it turned out that among their traditional value holdings, the manager owned a single stock—Qualcomm—that drove the entire 1990s outperformance. The manager, whose office was in California, caught on to the potential of San Diego–based Qualcomm's wireless patents early on, bought in, and let the position ride to become a huge part of the portfolio. Not only did they do a great job in buying Qualcomm, they did a great job in selling it—liquidating near the top and reallocating into their traditional value portfolio.

Let's make no mistake—this is a great achievement by the manager, and they deserve full credit for buying that stock and managing that position extraordinarily well. But what are the odds that they will have another Qualcomm in their portfolio in the future? Removing Qualcomm from their results suddenly made a spectacular manager appear quite average.

I'd much rather see performance driven by consistent application of a firm's stated strategy, even if it's not as impressive as the numbers generated by this Qualcomm-savant manager.

Next, beware the superstar manager. In my experience, most stars eventually burn out. Passive investment advocates will tell you that it's just as likely that an individual manager was lucky as it was that they were good. But it's also true that even if they were particularly skilled, things can change. And let's face it, in order to become a "star" you have to be exceptional, and that means taking big bets on assets and industries that inevitably mean-revert. I recall a long-term-successful manager telling me, "My goal is to be second quartile each year... the top-ranked managers need to take too many risks to get there." To clarify the investment-speak, the second quartile manager would rank in the 25 to 50 percent best out of the universe of managers. (This highlights a key difference between the investor's mindset and the entrepreneur's mindset. While every investor intuitively understands what this manager is getting at, you can see how this type of attitude can be incompatible with the entrepreneurial zeal to win.)

Success also brings its own challenges. It can be easier to manage a small portfolio than a large one, and so as a manager accumulates assets their strategy needs to adapt. It becomes harder to match past performance.

Over the years I've also heard stories about managers who lost their edge due to divorce or drug addiction. Both of these situations are more likely after experiencing a period of financial success.

There are countless ways that an individual's personal life will impact their investment results. How capable are you of making these judgments? How plugged in are you to know what's actually happening in their lives?

Another factor in the fall of many successful managers is hubris. Portfolio managers need to find a balance between having the confidence to believe they are correct while everyone else is wrong, and the humility to know when their analysis is faulty and they need to course correct. An extended period of success or acclaim can throw off that balance, over-loading the confidence side of the scale and resulting in a portfolio full of excessive risk and one-sided bets.

And then there are the specialized strategies pursued by hedge funds and niche managers. It's best to think of any strategy that relies heavily on manager skill and constant trading as a business in itself. That business is trading assets—stocks, commodities, currencies, and so on. Consider them as you would consider a direct investment in any other business. What processes are in place to ensure a consistent outcome? Who are the key people and what if something happens to them? And, most importantly—do you understand what they are doing to earn you a return on your money?

After you have considered all of that, let me ask you a question: Is researching a manager any simpler than researching a large public company? It sounds like there are a lot of variables at play, and they're not clearly reported to you each quarter like the results of that blue chip stock you own. You definitely need to do a bit of detective work to maintain full confidence. Do you even want to go there?

Among the firms presenting themselves as allocators, I've never seen one consistently able to choose top performers. They promise to build you a portfolio of the "best" managers in each asset class, but given all of the variables I've just described, I wonder if you're really just paying someone to over-diversify your portfolio for you.

Now, failure to identify outperforming managers in itself is not my biggest problem with the allocators, although I think they should be a lot more honest about their inability to do so. No, the greatest sin of the allocator is the extra cost involved in this management structure. You see, an allocator will have you paying two levels of fees—to the underlying managers, and to themselves at the top. I can virtually guarantee that they address this by telling you they negotiate lower fees with the managers you are allocating money to, and so the net cost to you is lower—not actually two full layers of fees. But that claim fails under any serious scrutiny, because if you are allocating to the "best" managers, what are the odds that those are the same managers who would be willing to cut their fees to collect assets from an allocator? Why would the "best" see the need to discount to attract assets?

Extra layers between you and your money are great for the HNW Industrial Complex. Are allocators promising to add value to your wealth plan in other ways that might justify their fees? Or are they just squeezing as much juice as they can from your portfolio?

The allocators also benefit from less accountability. "No pressure to consistently outperform," an allocator once explained to me over a beer. "Clients are a lot more forgiving when you're not the one actually managing the money. It's easier to just move money around and get paid for it."

Generally, for the investor, these arrangements work out just as you might expect they would. Some of your managers will do well, some won't. Occasionally, your allocator will recommend replacing one manager with another one, or adding a new strategy (all in the pursuit of "uncorrelated returns"). There is an illusion of incrementally moving towards a "perfect" portfolio made up of the "best" managers, but you will never actually get there.

So they've devised a great model that involves collecting fees on your money with no accountability for adding value. Amazingly, this industry has flourished in recent decades—a testament to the strength of a well-crafted sales pitch.

The Endowment Model pitch

Allocators tend to love stuffing portfolios full of prestige investments, justified by references to the Endowment Model, popularized in the early 2000s by David Swensen, manager of Yale's endowment fund.

Following a long period of exceptional performance by Yale's portfolio, it became all the rage to follow the model pioneered by Swensen, which grew the university's endowment fund over thirtyfold in a few decades, making it second in size only to Harvard's.

The model itself is based on having a lot of equity exposure—but not through traditional public markets. Over time, Swensen moved the fund from having the vast majority of its assets in public market stocks and bonds to having those assets make up only 10 percent of the portfolio. Where did the money go? Into all sorts of unlisted assets—hedge funds, private equity, private debt, venture capital, real estate, natural resources, and a host of other strategies and asset classes. Exotic stuff, inaccessible to almost all ordinary investors.

The Yale endowment was so successful that Swensen copycats arose everywhere... first in other Ivy League schools, then other nonprofits and institutions, and finally popping up in the private wealth realm, with packaged products that promised to deliver Yale-like returns to the everyman.

But here's the deal. Swensen was a genius. And he had a lot of capital to work with, many pre-existing relationships with excellent external managers, and a vast and capable team to help him implement the strategy. This is not easy stuff. And so the copycats have understandably failed to replicate the success of the Yale endowment.

However, that doesn't stop the HNW Industrial Complex from using it as a marketing gimmick. First of all, who wouldn't want to be associated with Ivy League schools like Yale and Harvard? This is instant marketing gold!

Second, the exclusivity factor is a huge draw for those marketing to the 1 percent. Not only are these strategies used by Ivy League schools, but, more importantly, the funds they're going to use in order to invest in these strategies are also accessible only to the wealthiest investors! The sales pitch often highlights access to managers you are only able to invest with thanks to the connections of the investment advisor (and the wealth of the other prestigious families with whom they work).

Aside from high fees, illiquidity, and complexity, another key fundamental problem with applying the Endowment

Model in the private client sphere is that the goals of institutions and their investment boards have nothing to do with the goals of individuals and their families.

Swensen himself is critical of the firms who have co-opted this strategy as a marketing tool. In his book *Pioneering Portfolio Management* he writes, "Consultants express conventional views and make safe recommendations. Selecting managers from the consultant's internally approved recommendation list serves as a poor starting point ... Clients end up with bloated, fee-driven investment management businesses instead of nimble, return-oriented entrepreneurial firms." He goes on to write that "active management strategies demand uninstitutional behavior from institutions, creating a paradox few successfully unravel."

So, in the very book he creates to let others know how he accomplished what he did at Yale, he basically explains why it will be extraordinarily difficult, even impossible, to replicate.

And while it's easy for foundation and endowment boards to remain emotionally detached from the process (they're investing other people's money, after all), it's much more difficult for private clients to do so. At the end of the day, not being able to sit down with the individual managing your money to ask questions and get answers about your life savings can be a frustrating experience. If my advisor is just a sales arm for a Bridgewater fund that is crapping the bed, I want to speak to one of the portfolio managers at Bridgewater, not a sales guy or a "relationship manager" who works for the firm.

And, frankly, Swenson was a unique talent who made something difficult look easy. In less capable hands, the Endowment Model simply doesn't work. In an October 2020 draft paper titled "Failure of the Standard Model of Institutional Investment," Richard Ennis concludes that large endowments have underperformed passive portfolios by 1.6 percent per year. His data notes that there was indeed a "golden age of alts," as he puts it, but this era lasted just a decade and a half and was ushered out with the 2008/09 financial crisis—precisely the time that asset managers began to peddle the Endowment Model to family offices and private investors as a way to counteract public market volatility.

Here's my recommendation: if anyone starts pushing the Endowment Model to you or starts talking about investing like an "institution," be very wary. They don't have Yale's resources. And you'll want to know what this strategy is costing you to implement all in. Without the Yale fund's scale, the costs of implementing these strategies would be proportionately higher, further cutting into your returns.

Ultimately, the Endowment Model has the potential to work for institutions. It checks a lot of boxes that help them achieve their particular objectives and give board members the cover they need from day-to-day market volatility. But for the private client, it's a marketing gimmick—one that far too many wealthy investors fall for.

Reduce the variables

So I've covered the problem of allocators and the institutional "endowment fund" sales pitch you are sure to hear, and I've explained why these portfolio solutions will often disappoint. But there is something more fundamental at work here—remember that earlier discussion around our preference for complex solutions over simple ones?

We are easily convinced that High Net Worth portfolios are supposed to be complex. It's what others do. It's what these high-end "multi-family offices" specialize in. Simple portfolios are for the common man, right?

But as a former allocator myself, I can tell you that there's a real challenge in building a portfolio this way. You see, deciding on allocations between managers and asset classes requires you to make a judgment on the relative attractiveness of an entire universe of assets—for example, increasing an allocation to stocks under the impression that they're "cheap." This is extraordinarily difficult to do, because at any given point in time there will be some stocks that are cheap, and others that are very expensive. When we talk about "the market" we're talking about the most popular, overvalued growth stocks, along with the defensive cash cow dividend payers. And so, no matter what the financial talking heads are saying at the moment, "the market" encompasses both the cheap and the expensive, the safer and the more risky. How hard is it to look at the universe of thousands of stocks and say with certainty, "stocks are cheap" or "stocks are expensive"? It's near impossible. There are simply too many variables at play.

So how should you build your portfolio? I've referenced the research, which shows that allocators fail to add value. But is there any truth to the claim that you should be diversifying your risk by hiring multiple managers? And, if so, how many different investment managers should you have? How much diversification do you need? What's the minimum effective dose?

There is a common perception that handing all of your money to one manager is risky. I'd say that depends on the manager. If it's a niche fund, or employs very complex strategies that depend on the skills of one particular individual, then I would agree with that assessment.

But if the firm you hire is sticking to the basics—building a conservative, diversified global portfolio for you—if they employ a low turnover strategy, and if they have a long track record of preserving capital, then I'd argue that it's not risky at all. And if they're looking to buy individual companies in your account, you don't have to try to predict whether "the market" is reasonably valued or where it's going to go next. No matter how frothy the general market sentiment, most managers will tell you that there's always *something* to buy.

So the answer to the question of how many investment managers you need is this: as few as you feel comfortable with, provided they are executing the right strategies. In a perfect world, you hire one very prudent manager and let them invest on your behalf. Give them direction to diversify around the world and across different industries. Give them freedom to ply their trade to the greatest extent possible. If you've made peace with the idea of missing out on what's hot and focusing on conservative, long-term investments, this should be all that you need.

I would add that having the majority of your wealth with one manager actually offers several benefits. They get to know you personally and understand your risk tolerance. They can optimize for your tax situation. You can take advantage of a sliding fee schedule as your portfolio grows. These factors may all be irrelevant to institutions, but they can be critically important to individuals and families.

If you do choose to have more than one firm manage your money, make sure that you identify one advisor as your "main" portfolio manager. It should be their responsibility to provide feedback on your overall asset allocation and coordinate over-lapping holdings in all of your different accounts. Make sure this person is someone you can trust to be impartial in their assessment of your other managers—ideally someone who already works with a lot of big clients and so doesn't *need* your business—which will allow them to provide honest advice.

To summarize, you can very easily build a very well-diversified portfolio. It's not as complicated as they want you to think it is.

You deserve an investment strategy built for individuals and customized for you. You are not an institution.

THE VOLATILITY
YOU CAN'T SEE
IS STILL THERE

"How did you go bankrupt?" Bill asked.
"Two ways," Mike said. "Gradually and then suddenly."

ERNEST HEMINGWAY

All-you-can-eat pizza and ice cream

I can hear the knives being sharpened as I write this. The HNW sales force will give you a number of reasons why you should be investing in prestige investments, a large subset of which they call "alternative assets." A recurring theme you'll hear is that they provide returns that are "uncorrelated" to the stock market.

The individual without a degree in finance might wonder what's so great about uncorrelated returns. I'll spare you the math, but basically this is the holy grail of finance. Adding an uncorrelated asset to a portfolio has the potential to simultaneously improve your returns while lowering your risk.

I can't put into words how excited this makes financial analysts. It would be like someone telling you that you can eat all the pizza and ice cream you want and never gain weight. It's that amazing.

How does low correlation work in the real world? Let's say you own a popular water park. In the warm months your business absolutely kills it. But the rest of the year's business can be pretty slow, and cash flow can be tough to manage. One way to address this is to acquire a nearby ski hill. The business peaks at the ski hill will be negatively correlated with the water park. Adding the ski hill to the water park will improve your overall returns. But what if it's a rainy summer and business at the water park is down? Well, then, maybe you want to add a movie theater to your portfolio—as people will be more likely to go see a movie on a rainy summer weekend. As you keep adding these low-correlation businesses to your portfolio, it strengthens your overall empire by diversifying your sources of cash. You can see how your total returns would go up, while your risk is reduced at the same time.

The way the math works out, your overall portfolio return improves when you buy an uncorrelated asset, even if it has a lower potential return than a different business that has a higher correlation to your existing portfolio.

We love uncorrelated returns. Higher returns. Lower overall risk. This is the proverbial "free lunch."

And so, invariably, the sales material produced by the alternative investment industry trumpets uncorrelated returns.

I recall meeting a sales guy for a private equity fund early in my career. "The asset class is uncorrelated to public markets" was one of his pitches.

"How is that possible?" I asked. "Let's forget what your charts and numbers say and think about this logically. Ultimately, in order to realize a return, the private equity fund needs to either sell the business or take it public. And so proceeds will be higher when public markets are doing well—there's a clear correlation. Not to mention the asset class's reliance on debt markets…"

This is now commonly acknowledged, especially after the private equity market buckled following the 2008/09 stock market collapse. But back then I was often told I was just being overly pessimistic and critical. You see, the numbers in the sales documents showed that public and private markets had experienced low correlations in the past.

But numbers lie. Private equity is not an uncorrelated asset. Since 2008, studies have demonstrated a consistent correlation of about 80 percent between public and private markets.

In fact, very few private market assets are truly uncorrelated with public markets. It's a trick of the data.

You see, private market assets are valued infrequently. At best once a month, but often only once a quarter or even every six months to a year. And these valuations require a lot of judgment, potentially ignoring factors that the valuation professional decides are temporary, or transitory. If you've been through a business sale process, I don't have to explain to you how valuation is more of an art than a science.

Meanwhile, your public market investments are granted no such grace. They are valued daily—in fact, multiple times each second—by the individuals trading them. These individuals are probably playing a very different game than you are—so their estimates of "value" may be quite a bit different from yours. (The "value" of a company's stock to a trader intending to flip the shares in a few hours is vastly different from the value calculation performed by a long-term investor.)

This gives private investments the illusion of low volatility relative to public market investments.

And so it's possible that two identical assets—one that trades daily on an exchange and one that is privately held and valued every six months by an independent valuator using a lot of judgment—show a low correlation to each other.

Investment consultants and prestige investment sales-people take this idea and run with it, creating portfolio illustrations that show the magical effect of adding alternatives to your portfolio. High returns and low volatility—basically magic.

I recall being in one meeting where a committee member stopped and asked the consultant, "If these numbers are accurate, why wouldn't we put 100 percent of the portfolio in alternative investments? Why invest in public markets at all?" The return versus volatility numbers were that compelling.

The consultant mumbled something about prudent diversification and limiting risk. What he didn't say—what the true answer is—is that *the numbers are wrong.*

They are made up. They are not comparable in any way.

Some alternative assets are uncorrelated. Most are not. Let's think through a few to demonstrate.

Hedge funds? If they actually hedge, maybe. Most don't. Research has shown that hedge fund indices are mostly pro-cyclical and correlated to the broader stock market. So most are just betting on the trend and the momentum in the markets. (The Guggenheim investment company estimates that between 2011 and 2020, hedge funds had a 0.81 correlation with the S&P 500—that's a meaningful statistic that indicates that there's not much actual "hedging" going on. Hedge funds and the markets actually move together.) And so rather than providing uncorrelated returns, they are just another risk asset in your portfolio, meaning that they move up and down with the stock market. Only this particular risk asset comes with much higher fees.

Collectibles? Wine? Art? Classic cars? Let's see ... who's buying them? Rich folk. Most of whom have their money in the stock market. If the market goes down, can they still afford the splurge? When the top 1 percent stop making extravagant purchases, look out below. There is a correlation to public markets, and it's real.

I could go on. But you'd be surprised how many "uncorrelated" assets are truly correlated to your stock portfolio in one way or another. There is a further problem: due to the unlisted and private nature of such investments, any data on these asset classes will always be incomplete and subject to cherry-picking by anyone with an agenda—whether they are trying to sell you something or, like me, trying to warn you away.

All I can say with common sense certainty is that if part of the sales pitch is uncorrelated returns, evaluate it with a good dose of skepticism.

Gradually, then suddenly

I will use a recent example to illustrate how private equity funds can hide what's really happening under the surface. Southland Royalty, an oil and gas producer owned by EnCap Investments, a private equity firm, collapsed in late 2019. This by itself is unremarkable. It was a tough environment for US energy producers. What's notable is how the collapse was reflected at the fund level.

As late as October 2019, EnCap valued their interest in Southland at $773.7 million. At the December report, the investment was marked down to zero. What happened in those fateful last two months? Nothing, really. Other than it became quickly clear that EnCap's valuation team had woefully overestimated the value of their holding in Southland.

It's derisively called "mark to myth" and "mark to make-believe" accounting, and it's a real problem for private assets that don't trade on an active market. It means there is often risk lurking that you don't see. It's fair to say that if Southland was trading on public markets, the price would have reflected the deterioration in its business as savvy money managers and insiders dumped their shares. Without that signal, you get a fund manager who believes that it's worth 99 percent of cost a mere two months before it goes bankrupt.

The reality is, though, that most of the time the volatility in a company's stock price doesn't result in bankruptcy. It bounces back. The storm passes. The cycle turns. And so while publicly traded assets *appear* to be more volatile than private funds, it's just an illusion.

Now ask yourself this question: Would you ever tolerate such obfuscation in your own business? Would you have survived over the years if you did? Would you allow your managers to fudge results and hide "temporary" impairments from you on the basis that they were short term in nature?

Of course not.

Now why do you allow it in your investment portfolio?

The illiquidity premium puzzle

One of the sales pitches you're sure to hear associated with prestige investments is that the illiquidity they offer is a *feature*, not a bug. You *want* the illiquidity, they'll tell you, because then you get to earn what the academic finance guys call an *illiquidity premium*. And because you may not need this money during your lifetime, or at least any time soon, you're crazy *not* to take on the illiquidity in order to earn the extra return.

In plain English, because illiquidity is an undesirable trait in an investment, those who are willing to take it on should be compensated for doing so. In practice, this means that illiquid investments are priced somewhat cheaper than they should be, meaning that investors will get higher returns by investing in them. So, for example, the theory says that if two investments pay off $100 in two years, the liquid one might be priced at $95, while the illiquid one (which you will be unable to sell) might be priced at $90. That incremental return you get paid for accepting this inability to sell is the illiquidity premium.

The finance world has done a lot of serious work over the years trying to figure out how much investors are typically paid for accepting illiquidity, with estimates I've seen ranging from zero to as high as 10 percent per year.

And then, in 2019, fund manager and researcher Cliff Asness dropped a bomb on the whole charade with a paper he titled "The Illiquidity Discount?" In this paper, Asness asks, "What if investors will actually pay a higher price and accept a lower expected return for very illiquid assets?"

Asness made the case that because illiquid assets are not being constantly valued by market participants, owning them may actually help long-term investors behave. That is, they hide the volatility you would otherwise see if your investments were publicly traded. As he says in the paper: "Many know that in private equity they're getting some serious smoothing, and a palatable (as it's way understated) reported volatility."

And so maybe one should expect a *lower* return in exchange for taking on illiquidity. In other words... maybe investors aren't buying illiquid investments at a discounted price. Maybe— just maybe—they're actually paying more for the "privilege" of not being able to panic sell their investments.

It's an intriguing thought experiment. I don't always agree with the conclusions Asness arrives at in his research, but he always makes me question my assumptions. This idea should force anyone chasing the illiquidity premium to question their own assumptions.

Volatility lies

John Maynard Keynes is famous for the branch of economics that carries his name. But few people know that he is also respected as a very successful investor.

In the paper "Keynes the Stock Market Investor: A Quantitative Analysis," Chambers, Dimson, and Foo deconstruct his investment track record as the bursar of King's College at Cambridge.

The short version is that once he stopped trying to time the market and transitioned his style to a more bottom-up value approach in the early 1930s, he kicked ass. His post-1932 record is one of consistent outperformance versus the benchmark.

Until Keynes came along, endowments had been invested almost entirely in real estate. He moved the King's College portfolio into public market equities, making the case that property investments were riskier than they looked.

> One must not allow one's attitude to securities that have a daily market quotation to be disturbed by this fact or lose one's sense of proportion. Some Bursars will buy without a tremor unquoted and unmarketable investments in real estate which, if they had a selling quotation for immediate cash available at each Audit, would turn their hair gray. The fact that you do not [know] how much its ready money quotation fluctuates does not, as is commonly supposed, make an investment a safe one.

So yes, private investments hide volatility. But just because volatility is hidden doesn't mean that it doesn't exist.

And seeing it doesn't mean you should succumb to irrational fear. Keynes's experience tells us that those who can manage their emotions and see through to what's really happening underneath the price action can position themselves for investment success... and it doesn't take a portfolio full of prestige investments to do so. Quite the opposite—he proved that by being able to see through the obfuscation of private markets and withstand the volatility visible in public markets, one can assemble a legendary investment track record.

12

THE VOLATILITY YOU CAN SEE IS LYING TO YOU

---

*I can calculate the motions of
the heavenly bodies,
but not the madness of people.*

SIR ISAAC NEWTON

The calm beneath the surface

The impact of a hurricane on the ocean's surface is a feedback loop. As the winds blow against the water, waves are formed. As these waves grow taller, they give the wind more surface area to press against, causing the waves to grow ever larger.

Below the surface, water is stirred up, and storms can be catastrophic for marine life that is not able to swim away or to greater depths.

But far deeper—200 to 400 feet below sea level, depending on the strength of the storm—waters remain calm. Submarines can safely pass underneath a strong hurricane provided they remain deep enough.

It's helpful to think of the prices of stocks as the ocean's surface. Usually calm, sometimes somewhat choppy, and occasionally in the grips of an extremely powerful storm.

These are the prices you see reflected on the evening news, the "stocks" app on your phone, or your online brokerage account. These are the waves.

Now think of the true value of the companies that you own as being the calm far beneath the surface. Yes, they will go up and down, but not by nearly as much as the turmoil we see on the surface.

And while the storm raging above is furious and loud, below there is calmness and peace.

The violence you see is masking relative serenity beneath the surface. It can provoke a visceral reaction in your mind, but focusing on it can cause you to panic and make mistakes. Instead, think of the calm beneath the surface and summon mental clarity and inner peace.

You might be riding into a hurricane, but you have the option to avoid letting it knock you off course. Get in a submarine, and ride it out from the calm of the deep. If built properly, it will get you through.

Don't confuse the market price with the value of the underlying companies.

Don't let market volatility knock you off course. It doesn't have to.

Boring is better

Volatility isn't always something we instinctively avoid. Sometimes we seek it out, because it can be thrilling.

In a 2007 matchup between the Dallas Cowboys and the heavily favored New England Patriots, Dallas held a tenuous four-point lead in the second half. The Cowboys were backed up first and twenty on their own ten-yard line. Not ideal, but they would have at least three chances to gain the twenty yards needed for a first down and to dig themselves out of a hole.

Running back Marion Barber took a handoff from quarterback Tony Romo about five yards behind the line of scrimmage, and immediately ran into a scrum on the left side. Most runners would have simply pushed their way into the scrum and taken what they could get before they were inevitably dragged down.

But not Marion the Barbarian. Rather than trying to push through, he spun his way away from a tackler. Almost immediately, two more Patriot defenders were on top of him, now pushed back to his own goal line. He was in danger of being tackled in the end zone, giving up a crucial two points to the Patriots. Breaking the first tackle, he evaded the second by running *backwards* farther into the end zone, while giving himself enough room to break free and run to the right side of the field. He proceeded to break *three* more tackles on his way out of the end zone as he picked up speed and ran along the right sideline.

Imagine this thrilling sequence in your mind. Search it up on the internet if you have the time—it's worth it! The comments on the YouTube clip include "top 10 greatest runs in NFL history," "the greatest 29 second video ever," and "unquestionably my favorite play in NFL history."

Barber was finally pushed out of bounds at the ten-yard line, pretty much where the ball was originally snapped.

Net gain on the play: two yards, according to official statistics, but in reality it looked like he was lucky to have gained a yard.

It was a high-risk play by Barber. Had he gone down where he met the initial scrum, the Cowboys would have lost minimal yardage. His attempt to make something out of nothing, to run back into the end zone looking for space to run, was a risky one because he could have given up a safety. Thrilling to watch, but risky. His coaches were almost certainly not pleased.

Lots of drama.

Lots of excitement.

But essentially no progress towards the goal of moving the Cowboys towards a scoring play.

So it is with stock market volatility.

The most volatile stocks attract the headlines, and therefore a disproportionate amount of novice investor attention. But playing in these stocks is risky, and while it might be exciting, they won't necessarily help you progress towards your goal. Worse, you risk losing significant ground in moving closer to your objective.

In an effort to make something out of nothing, Barber risked handing the Patriots two points (bringing them to within a field goal of winning) and giving their high-powered offense (led by Tom Brady) the ball back. But in that split second, Barber decided to break the rules, primarily based on his belief in himself and his ability to evade the Patriots' defenders. You might say that his decision was somewhat... entrepreneurial.

And while the entrepreneur can take those risks—hell, the entrepreneur often has no choice in the matter—the investor needs to behave more like the coach on the sideline, evaluating the odds and acting accordingly. If you watch the clip of Barber fighting his way back to the line of scrimmage, you see his sheer determination—he gave it everything he had and willed himself out of that end zone.

The entrepreneur does this routinely, but the investor cannot. Remember Warren Buffett's famous quote: "Rule number one: Never lose money. Rule number two: Never forget rule number one." It means that if you can choose between multiple options, you should always err towards the one that bears less risk of permanent loss.

Volatility is, in fact, a sort of tax on your returns. Because if you lose 10 percent, a subsequent 10 percent gain won't get you back to breakeven. That would require a gain of 11.1 percent. The secret to Buffett's long-term investment record is not that he consistently outperforms the market in good years, but rather that he loses less than the market in bad years. That alone can result in long-term outperformance.

So the risk with volatile portfolios is that you can dig yourself a hole that is very difficult to recover from.

Now back to that electric Marion Barber run. If you have a portfolio made up of those kinds of plays, it will be very exciting and fun to watch. But you'll occasionally take a big loss. You'll give up a safety. You'll be lucky to make it back to the line of scrimmage. And only rarely will you break that kind of run for a touchdown.

Don't get lost focusing on the volatility. Sure, it can be exciting, but the only number that matters is the yards gained on the play. If your objective is to win, in football or in investing, boring is better.

Holding through apocalypse

"If only I had invested in Amazon," you may have uttered at one point or another.

Let's play a game. Let's pretend you did.

If you invested in the company at any time in the 1990s, you were subject to severe drawdowns—on a few occasions seeing 50 percent of the value of your investment in the company disappear. You would have had to hold on through those drops. But they were just an appetizer for what was to come. The dot-com bubble popped in March of 2000, but there was no quick bounceback like the ones you had become accustomed to. Instead, the stock continued to sink. Every attempt to rally was met with more selling. There was no sign of a bottom and the stock price drifted lower... you were down 50 percent, then 60 percent, then 70 percent.

As traders tried to catch a bottom in the stock price, they were reminded of that old bit of dark stock market humor—that every stock down 90 percent was once a stock down 80 percent...that was again cut in half.

So what awaited investors next, while stocks struggled to recover ground lost in the crash? Only the horrific events of September 11, 2001, which shocked the world while shaking confidence in the economy and the stock market.

There was a capitulation of sorts, with investors fleeing all stocks, but particularly those that were perceived as more risky. And thanks to a high valuation and a lack of profits, Amazon fell handily into that bucket.

On September 29, 2001, the shares reached a nadir, down 95 percent from their peak in December 1999.

Let that sink in. Down *95 percent*.

Even before the public experienced the horrors of 9/11 and the uncertainty it would bring, investors were questioning the path the company was on. A *Bloomberg* article published not long earlier quoted a hedge fund manager who had the following to say about the company: "They're still losing money and are likely to continue to do so for the foreseeable future," and "It's up in the air whether their business model will work."

Barron's in 1999 featured a famous "Amazon.Bomb" cover story in which they called Amazon "just another middleman, and the stock market is beginning to catch on to that fact."

So you're holding on to Amazon. You think you're a believer in the business model and the leadership. But you're reading this kind of commentary in the media. And you've watched almost your entire investment in the company evaporate into thin air.

Did you keep holding?

Did you buy more?

Or more likely, at some point during the inexorable decline, did you decide you were wrong, capitulate, and sell it to end the pain?

Maybe you had the fortitude to hold it all the way down. Let's be honest. As it clawed its way back up, you very likely sold, happy to recover 10 percent, 20 percent, or 30 percent of the capital you put in, just glad that you were able to sell it for something.

Did you really think that the company would ever recover its peak? A stock down 95 percent has to go up 20x just for you to break even. And this is a company burning money every quarter, that other investors were giving up on en masse. Was a 20x return realistically in the cards? Did anyone without the last name Bezos actually survive the crash and faithfully hold all the way back up?

This is another reason why volatility is a killer.

It leads you to make horrible decisions.

If you can ignore it, as I implored in the previous chapter, that would certainly help. Some volatility is easier to ignore than others, though, and a 95 percent decline in a company that the mainstream financial media are expecting to fail is hard to ignore for almost everyone.

Even better than putting yourself in a position to have to ignore extreme volatility such as this is avoiding it in the first place.

Yes, if you bought and held Amazon stock you may have had a lot more financial wealth today. But the odds that you would have done so are essentially zero. If you held a portfolio of less volatile stocks that were already profitable, the chances that you would have held through the downturns are far higher.

I like to say that the only two numbers that matter are the price at which you buy and the price at which you sell. But the path between those two points can make all the difference in whether you're able to hold on for the long run. When you buy one of these crazy expensive stocks on the promise of future growth, you need to be prepared to hold through 90 percent drawdowns. It's not an easy mental space to be in, but it's what you need to do if you're buying for the long run.

Professional investors struggle with volatility as much as anyone. The only difference is that they're aware of it and try to take steps to mitigate it. I got a kick out of a recent interview with investor Jim Rogers. When asked how he focused on long-term outcomes, he replied to the interviewer, "I don't pay attention. Once I was investing somewhere, I think in an African country. The broker asked how often I wanted to receive reports. I said, 'Never send me any prices. I don't want to know. Because if they go up, I might sell. And if they go down, I might panic and sell. I don't want to know. I'm making a basic, fundamental, long-term judgment here that I expect in a few years this is going to make a lot of money. So don't send me the prices.'" Speaking about another one of his positions, he said, "I couldn't tell you the price of Aeroflot today. And I don't want to know. Don't tell me."

I'm telling you to ignore the deception of volatility, but as you can tell from Jim Rogers pleading with his broker, it's easier said than done. It's instructive to see the extent to which he is willing to go in an attempt to overcome his weaknesses—weaknesses that we all share. Compare this to the investment committees who grade portfolios every three months, or the investor who checks his portfolio performance each day (or multiple times each day!). Understand how harmful those activities are, and how they leave you susceptible to making mistakes. Remember the feedback loop we talked about at the opening of this chapter? Market prices can create a similar feedback loop in the investor's mind. The news is bad, and stock prices are falling, which confirms your fears, which causes investors to sell, which sends stock prices lower. The mental process of breaking that feedback loop is difficult for even the most experienced investors.

God would get fired

The extent to which portfolio swings and drawdowns can fake you out was perhaps best illustrated by Wesley Gray in a 2016 article titled "Even God Would Get Fired as an Active Investor."

Gray theorized an omnipotent hedge fund manager ("God"!) with perfect knowledge of the next five years. Knowing perfectly well what subsequent five-year returns looked like, his long-term record was amazing—holding the 500 best stocks, he compounded at just under 29 percent per year.

But the journey wasn't quite so smooth. Along the way, even this "perfect" portfolio was subject to dramatic drawdowns. It lost 76 percent between 1929 and 1932, and over 40 percent from 2008 through 2009, to give you two examples.

Even with perfect knowledge of what was to come, and even with an absolutely amazing long-term investment track record, the volatility was gut churning.

Let's face it—a nervous investor would probably have fired God.

An investment committee almost *definitely* would have fired God.

Yet another reason to filter out the noise of volatility if you can.

Remember that the price volatility you see is often lying to you.

It's the waves on the surface that you can easily glide beneath if you choose to.

It's the dramatic run that ultimately nets zero yards.

It's the price signal that leads you to sell when you should be buying.

Once you make peace with the idea that the same volatility exists with your unlisted private investments—it's just that you can't see it there—then you are that much closer to ignoring it when looking at your public market investments.

Volatility lies.

13

KEEP IT SIMPLE, KEEP IT LIQUID

Simplicity is the ultimate sophistication.
PROBABLY NOT LEONARDO DA VINCI

The venture lottery

One of the areas that open up for you if you're wealthy is private equity. Not only in the form of funds, but, more interestingly, also in the form of direct investments in the companies themselves. Most often, this involves early-stage venture investing. Why? Because these are the companies out there raising funds. More mature, profitable private firms are self-financing, and those looking to raise capital can do so through institutional investors on more favorable terms, rather than going directly to private individuals.

Let's say for a moment that there's an exclusive investment that not just anyone can get into. You have to know someone. Also, they're not accepting any checks below $150,000.

There are some other really famous investors who are in it. Maybe a few names you hear on CNBC. Maybe a few really high-profile local people you'd love to network with. You might run into them at the shareholder meeting!

Imagine if you had invested in Google before the IPO! This company might be the next Google!

The founders are brilliant. One of them is the guy who invented the Amazon "Buy It Now" button!

Let's face it, this is exciting. I just made up this fictitious company, and even I would be excited about investing in it.

Being an investor on the ground floor of a rocket ship, hitching your wagon to the next all-star CEO, and celebrating success with a close-knit group of investors sounds thrilling. And it's great cocktail party fodder. Is it any surprise that this is a huge attraction for entrepreneurs with liquid wealth?

However, this area is the Wild West of investing. The rules are different. The stakes are higher. And your dreams rarely match up with reality.

When a publicly traded stock investment goes bad, you can sell the stock, take a loss, and wipe your hands of the whole fiasco. But when a private investment goes off track, you can find yourself stuck. Worse, if you are the "deep pockets" in the investor group, you may be called upon to provide emergency financing to rescue the company (and to protect your initial investment).

In business school they teach you that the legal corporate ownership structure means that creditors can't go after shareholders beyond the value of their investment in the company. So as a shareholder, your theoretical maximum loss is 100 percent. When it comes to private equity, and the potential need to fund future equity rounds, your ultimate losses might actually turn out to be several times your initial investment. I've seen this play out many times.

Being a minority investor in the wrong private company can be a unique form of torture. Your rights are limited. Your ability to sell is limited. I've watched founders fight each other, watched C-suite leadership fight with engineers, and watched CEOs lose their jobs and set up a competing company the next day. All with shareholder money on the line. If you own a minority stake in the company while all of this is happening, you may have no choice but to sit by and watch helplessly as the drama plays itself out. Sometimes it happens behind the scenes, and all you hear are rumors and whispers, leaving you unable to find out what's really going on. Or, perhaps worse, you get entangled in the political struggle between the warring factions. I know more than one "retired" investor who had to unretire to take over a floundering investment after leadership abandoned the project. It's not fun.

Following high profile investors into venture investments is also a common mistake. You might have a few such investments in your portfolio, but you need to realize that the person whose coattail you're riding on might have hundreds of such investments, and expects the vast majority of them to fail.

Let's use the example of Masayoshi Son, head of Japanese firm SoftBank, who has tech investments around the globe. A *New Yorker* article quoted a former SoftBank executive as saying, "Venture capital has become a lottery. Masa is not a particularly deep thinker, but he has one strength: he's devoted to buying more lottery tickets than anyone else."

Early-stage private equity sounds exciting, sexy, and profitable. It can be all of those things. But more likely it will be none of those things. It can be a headache, involve costly legal battles, and tie up your cash for years, even decades.

And the investment performance? Well, it's a mixed bag. The best can do very well, thanks to connections and a platform through which they can promote their investments. Most others struggle mightily. The dispersion of returns is huge. At the end of the day, these are all just very expensive lottery tickets, and implementing the strategy properly means that you need to own a lot of them. It's hard to do this as a side gig, or as a non-institutional investor allocating a limited amount of money to the area for "uncorrelated returns." Seasoned angel investors can enter into hundreds of deals over the years, and so I implore you: understand the commitment you're getting yourself into. It's a full-time business … and a messy one at that.

Investment legend Charles D. Ellis summarized it nicely in an interview with *Bloomberg*: "Usually 90 percent of the great successes in venture investing go back to those same ten or dozen organizations. And success breeds success, which breeds success. So you're either one of the favorite investors, or you shouldn't consider venture investing, because you will not succeed."

I hate to sound overly negative, but it's best to approach the idea of investing in private companies, especially early stage and venture, with your eyes wide open. If after reading all of this you are still raring to go, then you might be the type of person who should be doing this type of investing. Go for it! As always, I advise my clients to limit their exposure and to make sure that the bulk of their wealth is in a safe basket of mature equities.

Avoiding rotten tomatoes

If you can't resist the excitement of this type of investing, what can you do to minimize the potential damage?

First of all, stay within your circle of competence. Unlike with public market stocks, if you decide you've made a mistake, it's likely impossible for you to exit for anything near what you initially invested. And that raises the level of difficulty several notches.

Second, realize that the area is a minefield. There are countless examples of wealthy individuals who have been bamboozled out of millions. Private companies are great for this, since they offer a unique way for scammers to circumvent investor protection rules. Cash can be misappropriated under the guise of business losses, and investors can be asked to pony up additional funds to protect their initial investment. Only invest in people you know and trust.

Third, keep amounts committed small. Try to negotiate some liquidity for your shares in case you decide you'd like to sell one day. And enter into it with a pessimistic assumption that you will lose everything ... because you likely will.

There are countless stories of private equity investments gone wrong. Athletes are notorious for falling into these schemes, as the combination of sudden money, youth, and inexperience in financial matters is a perfect storm for losing vast sums.

Former NFL quarterback Michael Vick is one example—he was unable to repay $6 million in loans he used to finance a car rental business, a wine enterprise, and other ventures.

Athletes are so often victims of scammers and shitty investments that ESPN's *30 for 30* documentary series devoted an entire episode to this phenomenon. Financial advisor Ed Butowsky was interviewed as part of the episode, and he told the story of an unnamed athlete who wanted to invest in a farm that produced giant tomatoes. The segment was played for laughs. He quoted his client: "Don't forget, Ed, there's tomatoes in ketchup, and everyone eats ketchup!"

While I'm watching this, I can't help but think of an extremely successful entrepreneur I knew who had invested significant sums in a company that was building an entire business with a very rich valuation around mini tomatoes, dehydrated for easier shipping. Not surprisingly, it worked out about just as well as the giant tomato business.

There's something about world-changing companies and entrepreneurs ... early on, their goals might sound ludicrous. Over time, they shape reality to their vision. But we know that the other side of risk tells us that the vast majority of companies attempting to change the world fail. As investors, we often look back and ask ourselves: "What on earth was I thinking?"

Look, I understand the attraction of direct private equity, and in particular venture investing. I've done it myself. It can be fun and exciting. In particular, many entrepreneurs feel like they benefit from having it as a focus after the sale of a business. One person I spoke with talked about how antsy he gets when he doesn't have a big project he's part of. Having one gives him an outlet for his energy. It gives him focus and calms him down. There are people who need this.

If you're well connected, well informed, and want to place a bet on an up-and-coming entrepreneur who's looking to rewrite the rules of an industry, go for it! Just enter into it with your eyes open and find ways to limit your risk. But be honest with yourself—is this really what you want? If you've got this nervous energy, is another startup the way to utilize it, or should you be looking for other outlets—whether in philanthropy, through mentoring, or by sitting on corporate boards? There are many ways to add value that don't involve putting your hard-earned capital at risk.

Collecting sour grapes

During periods of excess optimism and market froth, collectibles often become a hot topic in the "alternative" investment space. These hold a huge attraction, because, let's face it, it seems more interesting than stocks.

It's notable and newsworthy when a 1962 Ferrari 250 GTO sells for over $48 million, or a 1945 bottle of Romanée-Conti sells for $558,000. It grabs attention, particularly among those of us who lust after these cars, or would love to taste just a sip of a rare vintage. It was inevitable that someone would package and sell a fund that also invested in these items.

These collectible funds are not often widely marketed, and so it's hard to say what asset class kicked off this trend. The first I encountered was a fund that invested in vintage French wines.

These funds can proclaim several advantages for the long-term investor.

First of all—scarcity. You know for sure that nobody is going to be able to manufacture another bottle of 1945 Romanée-Conti. The bottles that exist will be damaged or, hopefully, enjoyed with an amazing dinner. And so supply will shrink over time. Scarcity value will only go up.

Then comes the idea that as more and more of the world obtains excess wealth, demand for the finer things will correspondingly increase, further pushing up values.

And significantly, collectibles are marketed as "uncorrelated" assets. You'll recall from our earlier discussion how attractive it is to own an "uncorrelated" asset, but you will also recall that this classification is often bullshit. Yes, collectibles don't trade daily and therefore don't show a high correlation to public equities. However, their values will tend to track the overall economy—specifically the wealth of the top 1 percent. The stock of global auction house Sotheby's, before it was taken private in 2019, was widely followed as a leading economic indicator. When rich people are buying up collectibles at ever-higher prices, times are good. So the idea that the values of these assets are "uncorrelated" with the stock market is more than a bit of a stretch. In fact, given that they are most often luxuries and not necessities, their prices will tend to be more volatile and subject to declines.

Finally, they offer the individual investor a chance to own a diversified portfolio. So rather than owning one painting or one car—along with being responsible for insurance, storage, and upkeep—you can own a small piece of several items, reducing your risk.

If you've followed my thinking on prestige investments up to this point, you're waiting for me to expose the catch to these funds. You might even be way ahead of me in identifying all of the potential issues they carry with them.

High fees? Check.

Illiquidity? Check.

Opacity? Check.

Bullshit historical performance and correlation numbers? Check!

Most of all, there's a tremendous amount of complexity hiding in what on the surface appears simple. Sure, it's art (which always goes up in value, right?), vintage wines (of which there is a limited and ever shrinking supply), or whatever other collectible you may be considering. It's all rather simple, isn't it?

Except it's not simple at all. Valuing a stock or a rental building, is relatively easy because these assets (generally) produce cash flows, which you can apply a discount rate to in order to determine a value. In the case of art, for example, who judges which painter becomes famous, and which is forgotten by history? Who determines which of those painters' works are most valuable?

Barron's writer Jack Hough explains the situation humorously... and also perfectly:

> Take Mark Rothko, who died fifty years ago. He is known for wall-size canvases filled only with hazy boxes of color... In 2014, a Rothko with three hazy boxes sold for just over $4 million—or about $1.3 million per box. The thing is, that same year, a two-box Rothko reportedly owned by Microsoft co-founder Paul Allen went for $56 million. The price-to-box ratio seems off to me.

Essentially, you're back to trusting the skill of an individual manager to choose the right works of art (or the right bottles of wine or the right collectible cars...) and they aren't necessarily going to be making the right bets.

And I haven't even talked about the issue of counterfeits, which is a serious problem that becomes worse as technology enhances the ability of criminals to produce very credible knockoffs.

It all comes down to the same issue I have raised many times in the past. If you're investing in one of these funds, you're investing in a business—in this case, a business created to invest in collectibles. And you're relying on the skill of the people managing that business.

Given the high cost, illiquidity, opacity, and potential for any number of things to go wrong, why would you choose to invest in this business rather than one that is more established, has a history of success, and trades on a public market, with all of the transparency and liquidity advantages that go along with it? Oh, and it doesn't charge you a management fee, either.

If you like wine, then build a wine cellar and enjoy your collection.

If you enjoy art, visit the world's great museums. Adorn your walls with pieces that are meaningful to you.

Best to keep these assets out of your portfolio.

There is no need to follow the wealthy crowds into exotic asset classes. You might not have interesting investment stories to regale the crowds with at your next cocktail party, but the freedom of a low-cost, fully liquid portfolio should outweigh that.

You've built your career on doing your own thing successfully. Why start following the crowd now?

Hedging against profits

By now I feel a bit like I've been beating a dead horse, and I'm sure you can see why the HNW Industrial Complex is so eager to sell you prestige investments.

Ultimately, we make money in the wealth management business in one of two ways. If we're charging a fee as a percentage of assets under management, we can either charge a lot, or ensure we retain the client assets for a long time. Even better if we can do both!

And so what if I could convince you that I've built something that is supposed to provide "uncorrelated returns" over the "long term"? You couldn't get mad at me for not keeping up with a rising market, because it's uncorrelated, remember? My product is designed to decrease your overall portfolio risk.

So this segment of your portfolio will likely stumble along over the years... not losing too much, not making too much. Just enough "uncorrelated" returns to cushion portfolio volatility.

This is how most hedge fund products work—especially a hedge "fund of funds" that your banker or family office professional may have sold you. By combining all sorts of different strategies into a fund and telling you not to expect it to outperform, they are ensuring that you'll have this miserable little fund in your portfolio for several years—maybe forever. And you'll forget what it is every year and ask your advisor and they will say, "Oh, that? That's there for risk management. It's uncorrelated." And you'll nod your head and move on.

They'll appeal to your ego, emphasizing how special you are, and how not many people can access this great investment. You're going to feel like a VIP. You've been told that you are in an exclusive fund with a high likelihood of strong investment performance.

Because there is no public market for the investment, it is going to be valued infrequently, so you won't see daily volatility in prices. This will also give you a false sense of calm.

Is it any wonder that the "multi-family office" world is full of these complex arrangements?

I generally prefer to access these investments through public markets—for example, you can easily invest in real estate, infrastructure, and even esoteric asset classes like litigation finance through fully liquid public vehicles. You can do so at a fraction of the cost, *and*—even better—many of these public companies are the actual management companies earning the fees that other investors are paying on those private funds you passed on.

An entrepreneur I know has a solid philosophy: if you like the asset class, invest in the managers, not in the funds. He has enough investible wealth that if he's approached by an alternative asset fund and likes what he sees, he'll offer to invest a significant sum ... as long as they also give him the opportunity to acquire equity in the management company. He'd rather collect the fees than pay them.

The HNW Industrial Complex has created a marketing machine driven around a perception of exclusivity and buzzwords promising a level of service and attention they are often unable to deliver. And so again I implore you: before buying into the marketing hype, look for professional credentials. Look for relevant experience. Look for an honest professional you can trust. Don't let anyone make you believe that, if you're not investing in their special funds, you are missing out.

14

PLAY YOUR OWN GAME

Investment is most intelligent when it is most businesslike.
It is amazing to see how many capable businessmen try to operate
in Wall Street with complete disregard of all the sound principles
through which they have gained success in their own undertakings.

BENJAMIN GRAHAM

Following the wealthy crowd

The reader of this book has likely been approached at one point, or will be approached eventually, by one of several High Net Worth or family office "peer organizations," the purpose of which is often advertised as bringing together wealthy investors to share ideas and experiences.

The objective is noble and there's certainly a need for this type of organization. However, I'm about to explain why you need to be very careful when considering participation.

You generally won't hear professional money managers say anything bad about these membership groups. They are an excellent source of prospects and a great sales funnel if you're invited to participate. And I could probably sell a lot of copies of this book to such groups if I write a chapter on how great they are.

But if you've read this far, you know that I am nothing if not honest.

These organizations can be quite helpful in that they can provide a peer community for wealthy individuals who have outgrown past relationships, or who maybe don't have anyone to turn to for help with new challenges presented by wealth.

Getting recommendations on professionals or creating a network of families facing the same challenges as you is a huge benefit, and I applaud these organizations for creating a forum where this is possible.

The problem begins when they venture into the investment realm. Not only are members encouraged to share "opportunities" with each other, some also promote a "portfolio defense," in which members present their portfolios to their peers for critique.

No doubt the room is filled with successful entrepreneurs. Brilliant minds. Innovative thinkers.

But not investors.

Remember how one of our biases is that we have more respect for complexity than simplicity? Imagine how a large portfolio of publicly traded stocks would fare in such a defense, versus an Endowment Model-type portfolio. I can almost guarantee that the person who shows up with a basket of blue-chip stocks will be encouraged to diversify by exploring private deals and alternative investments. By now, you know how I feel about that.

One such organization's marketing material says that the purpose of the defense is to "harness the collective intelligence of the group" to help the member construct their portfolio. This sounds awesome, until you remember that the consensus in investing is so often wrong. Outsized returns are earned by investors with a different view of the world, who happen to be right. Following the crowd (or letting them influence your thinking) is a recipe for marginal results, at best (and absolute failure, at worst).

And then there's the implicit respect that some people in the room will command. The newly wealthy, like the layperson, often carry with them the impression that there are secret "keys to the kingdom" possessed by the senior members of the group. There is also a certain reverence paid to the more successful members. But there are no secrets. There are no keys. And there is no kingdom. The wealthy are just as lost as the rest of us. The supreme confidence of the successful entrepreneur so often hides the reality that they have no idea what they are doing—they are often making it up as they go along. Just like everyone else! The only difference is that they have the ability to command the confidence of those around them, regardless of how far off the rails they may be.

So peer learning groups are a great idea with serious limitations. Oh, and I haven't even mentioned the annual membership fee, which appropriately reflects the very high-end target market. Probably best to avoid these clubs and build your own network of people you know and trust. If you choose to join, keep in mind those limitations.

Simplify investing

Investing isn't complicated. The hardest part of it isn't the spreadsheets, the technical analysis, or the forecasting. The hardest part is actually maintaining discipline. And so having a framework guided by business principles gives you a huge advantage over other market participants.

Stripped to the basics, investing is doing one of three things:

1   Owning a piece of a company (or asset) by investing in its equity

2   Lending a company (or government) money by investing in its bonds

3   Pursuing one of many alternative strategies, the success of which are usually less about the investments and more about the specific skills of the asset managers

That's it. Any strategy you might pursue is some kind of combination of these three things.

Buying stocks? Private equity? Real estate? That's point #1. You're buying a piece of ownership. The goal here is generally growth—both in the value of your investment and in the dividends received.

Investing in bonds? Stashing money in a savings account? That's #2. Lending your money for a safer return. Remember, bondholders get paid first, so this offers more security than investing in equity. But, because of that, also lower expected returns.

And then there are all sorts of exotic alternative strategies that are pitched to wealthy investors. The prestige investments generally fall into this bucket. That's #3.

There. I've just covered over 90 percent of the investment universe for you.

Now the difficult part is what to do with this information. The number of choices you have to build a portfolio is endless—much greater than the actual number of investments you have to choose from.

The hardest part of investing isn't the technical aspects. It isn't even figuring out what to invest in. It's maintaining discipline. A simple strategy will help you do that.

A key message of this book is to keep your portfolio simple, and to reduce the variables at play. You already know that owning equity in your own company is what got you here. So you won't be surprised to hear me tell you that owning equities will be the centerpiece of a "stay wealthy" portfolio.

Old School investing

Back in the mid-twentieth century, the average person's stock portfolio consisted of large, well-known, dividend-paying corporate shares. There were no real-time stock quotes (you would need to wait for tomorrow's newspaper to see how your stocks closed today). Transaction costs were high, so there was very little trading in and out of positions. Most investors focused on clipping interest coupons on their bonds and collecting dividends on their stocks. Because you held for the long term, the vast majority of your savings were in companies like General Electric, AT&T, and Procter & Gamble. Companies that dominated their industries and promised to stand the test of time. Doesn't sound too exciting, does it?

Many of today's investment advisors would scoff at this portfolio, especially in the day and age when technology has given us the ability to invest globally in a wide variety of asset classes. Investors can now access private markets (equity and debt) and exotic collectibles fairly easily. These assets are no longer solely the purview of the very wealthy.

Is this a good thing?

Investment innovation has been called the democratization of investing, and how can democratizing anything be bad?

I suppose it means that, thanks to technology, the average investor now has just as much of a chance of incinerating capital in the art market as the wealthy.

I would hope that, given the ability for smaller investors to access just about any asset class a wealthy investor could access, this form of prestige investing is due to lose its cachet. Because—as I outlined in earlier chapters—it doesn't really work.

And yet ... people continue to believe that investing in blue chip equities is a dinosaur's game from a bygone era. There's a pull to be part of what is new and exciting. It's hard to seemingly be the only person who's not getting rich off the latest fad investment.

There is a tried-and-true method to building and preserving wealth, and it works.

I'm going to encourage you to be a maverick. Embrace the Old School.

Charlie Munger has famously said about investing, "If you think it's easy you're stupid." At one level he's right. If you're trying to get rich, investing is difficult. Even more modest goals, like outperforming a benchmark consistently, are really hard. But if you aren't worried about what the rest of the world is doing, if you're able to focus on keeping it simple and controlling your emotions, it actually isn't hard at all. You might even say it can be kind of easy.

Let me tell you a story about Dorothy, a client of an advisor I worked with very early in my career. She had grown up during the Great Depression, and like most from her generation, she respected the value of a dollar. She earned a modest salary and lived a modest life.

With no formal financial education, she built up a very significant portfolio by adhering to a couple of very simple rules.

First of all, she only bought stocks that paid dividends. She believed that kept management accountable about maintaining profits and managing cash flow.

Second, if a company cut its dividend, she sold it. She figured something must be wrong if they couldn't maintain the payment to shareholders—likely a deterioration in the business.

She ignored the financial news, didn't read the business section, and knew little about the world's macroeconomic environment. She invested through wars, recessions, investment bubbles, inflationary environments, and wild movements in interest and exchange rates. Nothing fazed her—concentrating on her dividends, she built up a multi-million-dollar portfolio.

Now, I'm not suggesting this is a strategy for everyone—it does have its flaws. But it worked wonders for her, and I'm sure that she outperformed the vast majority of people who spent their days searching for the next great undervalued stock.

If trying to outperform others is the game you're playing, it's very difficult to succeed. Charlie is right.

But if you can play Dorothy's game, or something similar, it's actually quite simple. Charlie's not playing this game. The pros are not playing this game. But there is no reason that you can't play this game.

Keep reminding yourself—

The institutions are not playing the same game as you.

The day traders are not playing the same game as you.

The money managers on CNBC are not playing the same game as you.

Build a portfolio that suits you. Ignore the noise. Play your own game.

15

THE MARKET IS
NOT YOUR FRIEND

*The main purpose of the stock market
is to make fools of as many men as possible.*
BERNARD BARUCH

The market as adversary

Many entrepreneurs I've worked with over the years are skeptical of the stock market and, by extension, of financial advisors. They've been burned in the past and won't let it happen again. As one entrepreneur memorably told me at our first meeting, "I hate you investment guys, and I hate the stock market."

And I can't say I blame him.

There's something about financial markets that exists only to make sure that short-term-oriented traders lose money. If you've ever played this game, you know how frustrating it can be.

Markets lull you into a false sense of security exactly when you should be most cautious.

Markets convince you that risk is at its peak at the exact moment when all the risk is reflected in prices, and you should be buying aggressively.

Someone with a bit more eloquence might say that the stock market's goal is to frustrate as many investors as possible. The collective actions of the crowd ensure that prices are highest when people are most optimistic, and lowest when confidence is at rock bottom.

But I'll just say that the market hates you. It is always out to separate you from your wealth.

Picture the stock market as a malevolent, horrible entity that wants nothing more than to see you separated from your savings. In that effort, it has recruited the financial media to help paint a picture that goes against everything you should be doing.

In *The Screwtape Letters*, C.S. Lewis tells the fictional tale of two demons—Screwtape and Wormwood—who use all of the temptations of our physical world and all the foibles of human nature to separate us from religious salvation.

The market is another version of Screwtape, using your own human nature to force you into making bad investment decisions.

Buying when you should be selling.

Selling when you should be buying.

The fact that the market hates you makes it hard to know what you should be doing at any given point in time. You can't reliably outsmart it, so you must maintain a defensive posture, anticipating an attack at any time.

C.S. Lewis illustrated the need to be aware of the tricks of the demons and to avoid them. I would say the same about the hyperbolic financial news, which can trick us into actions that go against our long-term objectives. And yet, even the best of us get sucked into daily market commentary, or debate short-term market moves.

The market is inviting you to play a game you can't win. Don't accept the invitation.

The illogic of trading versus the logic of investing

One of the frustrations of being a parent is that children can't be reasoned with.

No, you can't have ice cream for breakfast.

I know you're building a fort but can I have my couch cushions back?

Please stop feeding the dog my ribeyes.

With great difficulty, I'm learning that one of the keys to parenting is knowing what to let go and choosing your battles wisely. Once you give up the expectation that your children will act rationally, it becomes somewhat easier to deal with the fact that your humidor is now a treasure chest full of plastic gems, and your cigars are tree trunks floating down a Lego town "river."

The same thing applies to the market. To the outside observer, the stock market seems relatively simple. Good news, stocks should go up. Bad news, they should go down. But if you expect this, you are setting yourself up for disappointment. Here's a basic and important fact about the stock market: good news doesn't necessarily move it up, and bad news doesn't necessarily move it down.

Why doesn't it behave rationally?

It does . . . just not in the way you expect.

Think of it like the world's largest game of chess, with millions of investors jockeying their billions of pieces. You are competing against all of these people, all trying to anticipate what's coming around the bend and to be first in (or first out).

And so it is that the casual observer or stock market hobbyist wonders why their investment went down on good news, or up on bad news.

Well, it's because a lot of smart people may have already seen this news coming. To give you an example of how this is working, large investors can buy access to satellite and cell phone data that tracks customer activity at various retail locations. And so by the time your favorite retailer reports amazing earnings, those investors will have already made this determination, bought the stock several months ago, and will be selling their shares once the information is common knowledge.

We call this "selling on the news," and it's one of the most frustrating things the new investor deals with. In order for good news to move stock prices up, the news has to be *better* than most people expected. In a hot growth stock, that often means that there's a ridiculously high bar to clear.

And this also applies with bad news. Especially with bad news.

It seems like an investment advisor really earns their pay when they prevent clients from selling when all the news is bad. Because here's the thing: if it's really bad, *everybody knows it's bad!* There is no longer any point in selling, because prices should reflect how bad things are.

It's quite uncanny how many clients reach the point of maximum pain around the same time. Often, the phones start ringing and, within days of each other, clients beg to sell everything. This *always* happens at the wrong time. I've been doing this for a quarter century through three catastrophic crashes, and you can set your watch by it. Our collective psychology is really that predictable. When the phones start ringing with clients wanting to sell it all and end the pain, you know it's time to suck up the courage to buy.

In the business world, it's not enough to have an idea, or see a trend. You don't profit unless you act on it. Because of this, there are often opportunities lying in plain sight, only because others are too lazy, or they're preoccupied, or financing is tough to come by. But in the investment world, there is no such friction to trading on information. Unless you are seeing something that nobody else can see, *the price at which you are buying or selling usually already reflects the information leading you to buy or sell.*

It can be hard for entrepreneurs to wrap their heads around this, because they have spent their careers observing and reacting, adjusting business practices, pricing, or marketing in order to maximize profits. And the switch to investing does not offer that same opportunity. If you spend all of your time reacting to developments in financial markets, you are going to churn your account to death and will never earn the returns you're hoping for.

The multi-dimensional chess game aspect of markets simply makes it too difficult to attempt to adjust your portfolio based on what you are seeing in real time. It's probably hard for you to accept that the best move is often to sit still. It's not natural or comfortable. But it's what you need to do.

The reason for this is that, even with perfect knowledge of the future, you don't know how the market will react to different events. Nobody does. If you think you do, you're wrong.

The way to offset the whiplash of trying to trade based on short-term data and developments is to ignore it. Focus on the long-term and ignore the noise. In this way you can move beyond the manic and illogical short-term market moves and build a long-term strategy based on sound business principles, which are far easier to comprehend and anticipate.

Nobody knows anything

I remember watching CNBC back in 2003, prior to the eruption of the second Gulf War. The market was anxiously awaiting the beginning of the conflict as troops prepared for combat to begin. As is often the case at anticipatory times like this, the market was holding in a very narrow range, as traders hesitated to make any big bets. The news anchor was interviewing a New York Stock Exchange floor trader about the quiet before the storm, and the trader said, "We're just waiting for the bombs to start dropping." The anchor asked, "What happens then—buying or selling?" And the trader, in one of my favorite ever moments of television honesty, said, "I don't know. I'll just look around and see what everyone else is doing."

More recently, the leadup to the 2016 US presidential election saw all sorts of speculation about what would happen to the stock market if Donald Trump were to win. Almost nobody saw this as a positive scenario for the market—most of the debate was whether the market would crash 10 percent or closer to 50 percent on a Trump victory. And as election results began to come in, stock futures did in fact begin to plummet. In fact, they hit "limit down," which is a trading halt designed to give traders a chance to take a deep breath before hitting the sell button, hopefully stopping the panic liquidation in its tracks. The financial world braced for a stock market crash.

But then a funny thing happened. The next morning, futures started to rise. The market opened flat, and then proceeded to climb throughout the day. Frankly, nobody knew what was going on. But that didn't stop news outlets from breathlessly reporting how a Trump presidency would be great for business and great for stocks. These are the same people who just twenty-four hours earlier were dreading that very same prospect. So the narrative follows the price action.

Basically, nobody knows anything.

Not the big names being interviewed on CNBC. Not the celebrity fund managers. Or the investment bloggers. Or that snarky anonymous dude on Twitter.

Everyone is just making up explanations after the fact, making predictions based on their own biases, or talking up their own investment portfolio.

The sooner you come to realize that nobody knows anything, the easier it will be for you to ignore the noise.

Your partner in hitting home runs

What the casual observer fails to understand is that stock prices in "the market" are not objective. They reflect the aggregate judgment of all market participants. And so if all of the news coverage you are reading is negative, chances are that this will already be reflected in investor outlooks, and so prices will be low. Any news that is "less bad" than most people expect will therefore actually result in *higher* prices. This means that, counterintuitively, the worse the news is, the better a time it is to invest. In that sense, saying "I'm optimistic, because how much worse can things be" is not just dark comedy but a viable investment strategy.

Conversely, when everyone is optimistic about the future, prices are probably as high as they're going to get. A bright future is priced in, and so it will be hard for prices to continue to rise.

It's counterintuitive, particularly for the businessperson who is often used to following trends of consumer behavior. If everyone is thrilled about a product, you make money by giving them more of it!

Being an investor requires you to change your thought process, and to become more of a contrarian. Rather than chasing trends, investors need to look for areas where consensus opinion is wrong.

And so one needs to assume an almost adversarial relationship with the markets, and with financial news. It's important to develop an awareness that the news you are listening to is the exact same news that everyone else is also hearing. And so whether what you're hearing is negative or positive, remember that it's likely already reflected in market prices.

That the crowd is always wrong is an investment truism. The peaks of mania are times when everyone is loading up on margin debt and day trading. And the market usually bottoms just as everyone has given up hope and decided that prices will never rise again.

If this leads you to conclude that people are stupid, I'm not going to argue with you, just based on principle. But that's the wrong conclusion to arrive at. The crowd isn't wrong at market extremes because it's stupid. The crowd is wrong at market extremes because that same crowd is setting the prices at which it's buying and selling. If everyone is optimistic, prices are going to be too high. If everyone is pessimistic, prices will be too low. And so even if the crowd is right to be optimistic or pessimistic, once prices reflect that view, there's no incremental money to be made. You're just going along for the ride.

How to overcome this? Be comfortable buying and owning stuff that is out of fashion. The stock market is like a store that is constantly updating its prices to reflect worldwide demand for its products. The minute everyone decides they don't like black shirts (Shows dog hair! Too hot to wear in the sun! Fades in the wash!), the price of black shirts will fall. Eventually, you should buy those black shirts because they will get so cheap that it won't make sense to buy the pink shirts everyone else is wearing. Because, let's face it, a black shirt hides your belly, and it looks best with a pair of blue jeans, and the world will eventually come around to realizing that.

Every good investor needs to keep this in mind—that market euphoria and panic are really working against you to force errors. And despite me saying that the market hates you, I'm certainly not suggesting that you avoid it; quite the opposite, I encourage you to embrace it.

One of my favorite well-known quotes comes from the legendary Japanese slugger Sadaharu Oh, who said that he never saw the opposing pitcher as his adversary, but rather as his "partner in hitting home runs."

Sadaharu Oh would never have become the legend that he is without those opposing pitchers.

You need to look at the stock market in the same way.

Always remember: it is trying to defeat and deceive you. It is not on your side. But you can use it as your partner to hit home runs. Your partner to build wealth... and stock up on black shirts when they're on sale.

16

GET PAID TO TAKE RISK

*When you boil it all down, it's the investor's job
to intelligently bear risk for profit. Doing
it well is what separates the best from the rest.*

HOWARD MARKS

Don't take risk for free

I'll make you a deal.

We'll flip a coin. If heads comes up, I'll give you $2. If tails comes up, you give me $1. It's a no-brainer. You've got to take that bet.

Flip.

It's tails.

You lose.

I'll make you another deal.

Let's take this pack of playing cards.

Pick a card at random—if you pull the ace of spades, I'll give you $100. If you pull any other card, you give me $50.

Shuffle, shuffle. Grab your card.

It's the ace of spades—you win!

So I guess that the second bet was the smarter one. Good for you for taking it!

Of course, this is nonsense. You understand that you had the odds on your side for the first bet and way against you in the second bet.

Ideally, in the second bet you would have demanded at least 52:1 odds, since the odds of the ace of spades coming up are exactly 1 in 52 (assuming the jokers are taken out of the deck).

These principles are universal. We understand them when we're playing card games and betting on sports. Why don't we understand them when we apply them to investing?

This discussion has me recalling a chat with a friend who owned a small piece of a very successful private business and was debating cashing out to invest in public markets.

"How much would you expect to earn on a stock and bond portfolio?" he asked.

"Based on current values and interest rates, most likely you will see a mid-single digit return in the future."

"That's garbage. Why would I take money out of the business for mid-single digits when our long-term growth target is at least 8 percent?"

"Would you rather a lower risk 5 percent or a more risky 8 percent?"

"We'll probably make a lot more than 8 percent."

"OK, but for the sake of argument, let's say you only make 8 percent."

"Why would I choose 5 percent over 8 percent?"

"Because the range of potential outcomes is narrower."

"What are you talking about? Is there a time when we've ever made less than 8 percent growth over a few years? It's never happened. Where is the risk?"

"The risk was always there. You have been lucky not to experience it. Just because you don't see the risk doesn't mean it isn't there."

"I'll take the 8."

In comparing the 5 percent to the 8 percent, my friend neglected to consider the risk.

The 8 percent return was offered by a private business he did not control, with no liquidity to sell his shares, in a single industry, operating in a narrow geographic area. It was a relatively risky 8 percent.

The 5 percent was offered by a fully liquid, diversified basket of high-quality global assets, buffered by a bond portfolio that would likely actually go up in value in the event of a recession. The 5 percent return estimate was a conservative assumption, and, over the long term, a far more likely outcome than the 8 percent choice.

There is far less risk in the global public market portfolio. You would *expect* to earn a lower return in it than in the private company. But in my friend's mind, 8 percent is greater than 5 percent, and so he couldn't understand why he should choose to invest in the global basket.

Looking down the road, if there is a far wider range of outcomes in one investment over another, you need to demand a higher expected return from that investment.

I'm not sure what that premium is—there's no hard and fast rule, and it really depends on the specifics of each investment. But before you are seduced by a high projected return estimate, make sure to ask about the risk.

Sure, you might be looking at an investment that promises to pay you a double-digit return . . . but what is the range of potential outcomes? And how bumpy will the road be to get there?

Bottom line: risk matters. Make sure you're well compensated for taking it.

Don't take ace-of-spades risk without at least a 52:1 payoff. Get paid to take risk.

What's your benchmark?

Institutional investors worry a lot about how their portfolio performs against a benchmark. You're going to hear a lot about benchmarks if you start talking to consultants and high-end money managers.

Should it matter?

In a word, yes. But also, no.

It matters because you don't want a manager or advisor who hides their performance statistics. If it's difficult to see what your return was for the last quarter, or the last year, or since you opened your account, you can be pretty sure that there's a reason for that. They don't want it to be easy for you to see how your portfolio has performed. You need to demand transparency on this matter. I am consistently amazed at how many "high-end" wealth managers don't provide their clients with this basic information.

But performance numbers themselves don't tell the whole story. If your portfolio is up 15 percent, that sounds pretty darn good! However, if the stock market is up 25 percent over the same period, it sounds less good. But the analysis doesn't stop there. If your manager earned the 15 percent without taking a lot of risk, then it might actually be a pretty good return versus a much higher-risk 25 percent.

What does that mean? Well, if the market was instead down by 25 percent, but the portfolio created for you would only be down 10 percent in that same period, then you're probably happy to be in that lower-volatility portfolio, even though it means you don't fully participate on the upside. Protecting the downside is the key to long-term returns.

As you can see, there's a lot of complexity and no easy answers here. A lot of "it depends." Which is not terribly helpful, I know.

And that's also why benchmarks shouldn't matter that much to you. What should matter is whether you are able to meet your own personal objectives, not keeping up with other investors.

Shortly after a market crash, I proudly told a client that we had a good year. Our benchmark was down 15 percent, but his portfolio was only down 10 percent. Any financial professional would see that as a pretty good job protecting the downside!

Except the client didn't. He turned to me after my smug little summary of what a great job we did and said, "Don't ever tell me that it's a good year after you lost my money."

Message delivered.

The game of relative returns—the one that virtually the entire investment industry is organized around—doesn't matter to you. Nor should it.

It goes both ways. You don't want to lose money when the market goes down, and that means holding lower-risk investments. But it also means that if the market is in the midst of a high-risk speculative frenzy, you should be able to ignore the money everyone else is making.

It's hard to avoid the FOMO (that's the "fear of missing out" on a great party), I know. We often find ourselves second-guessing a conservative investment stance when speculation is rampant and it seems like every amateur day trader is making money. But resisting FOMO is critical to your long-term success.

So, what is the appropriate use of benchmarks then?

They're useful for evaluating a specific manager's performance. (Make sure you're using the right benchmark, because managers can often fudge this to make themselves look good.) But benchmarks are also horrible for tracking the success of your overall portfolio, because the market return is irrelevant to measuring progress towards your goals.

If you and your advisor determine at the outset that a 4 percent annual return will allow you to meet your objectives, don't chase a 10 percent return. You don't have to! Take it easy and sleep well at night. Your benchmark should be that 4 percent—and don't worry about the frenzy.

Professionals are subject to FOMO as well, and it's no joke. Legendary investor Stan Druckenmiller famously lost an estimated $3 billion in six weeks by investing $6 billion at the top of the 2000 technology bubble. In his own words:

> I just couldn't stand it anymore. And I'm watching them make all this money every day. For two days I'm ready to pick up the phone and buy this stuff... I pick up the phone and I buy them. I might have missed the top of the dotcom bubble by an hour.

Druckenmiller acknowledged the stupidity of what he had done and that it was driven purely by greed and FOMO.

> I bought $6 billion worth of tech stocks... and in six weeks... I had lost $3 billion in that one play. You asked me what I learned. I didn't learn anything. I already knew I wasn't supposed to do that. I was just an emotional basket case and couldn't help myself.

As you can see, this is ingrained in our human nature. If it's not easy for Druckenmiller, it's not going to be easy for any of us. The mindset shift is critical to make, and you need to keep reminding yourself what game you're playing. I want you to look forward to missing out on this year's hot stock, or the startup all your friends are invested in, or the cryptocurrency you don't really understand.

Overcome the FOMO. Stick to the long-term plan. Play your own game. This should be a strength of the entrepreneur. Your success is so often based on your individuality and refusal to follow the crowd.

I collected monthly large cap US stock returns going back to 1926 and decided to play around with the numbers.

Let's say your portfolio only captured 80 percent of the market upside (that is, if the market is up 10 percent, you are only up 8 percent), but with the benefit of only experiencing 50 percent of the downside (so if the market is down 10 percent, you are only down 5 percent). Over close to a century, you will end up with outperformance of just over 12,000 percent.

OK, that's a little bit extreme. Let's dial it back by giving up some upside.

If we capture only 70 percent of the upside, the outperformance over time is 993 percent.

I can live with these numbers.

You don't have to keep up with the market as long as you can control your downside.

Celebrate your ability to tune out the noise. Don't follow the crowd. Be a maverick. Set your own benchmark.

"I'm in Boca"

"Risk" isn't a term you would think needs to be defined, but in the investment world it's imperative that you clarify what you mean when you talk about risk.

Professor Elroy Dimson of the London Business School famously said, "Risk means more things can happen than will happen," which is a pretty good place to start. It sets the stage for any scenario where risk exists.

But for the businessperson or the individual investor, talking about risk usually comes down to the risk of losing money—that is, we're worried about downside risk as opposed to upside risk.

But even that simplified definition leaves questions.

To start, what's the time period you're talking about? If I won't need to cash in my investment for another twenty-five years, is it still risky if it's down a month after I invest? How about a year? How about five years? Obviously, if I'm down in year twenty-four, I have something to worry about. But somewhere between day one and day 9,125, I have to have an investment that is at least earning me a positive return.

Positive return. Hmm. So if you invest $1,000 today, and you have $1,001 in ten years, is that a positive return? Would you be happy with that?

It depends!

If inflation has averaged 2 percent per year over those ten years, you have lost money. After accounting for inflation, you have lost purchasing power. You may have a positive *nominal* return of $1, but your *real* return is negative.

But if prices *fell* over ten years (that is, there was deflation), then you might just be happy with that $1 nominal return.

So, maybe risk is really about maintaining your purchasing power over time.

That's a better definition, but we're still not quite there yet.

The average investor would agree that they at least want to maintain their purchasing power, and so define risk as failing to achieve that. That's at a minimum.

But if you're invested in risky assets, such as stocks, you need to be doing better than that over time; otherwise, it's hard to justify the risk you're taking (and the risk in equities is that your holdings go to zero). This is called "risk adjusted return," and it's a critically important concept that most non-finance types have never really considered.

So, this all seems quite logical so far. If I'm going to invest, I want to get paid to assume risk. Risk is my partner in hitting home runs. It's why I expect to earn a positive return from investing!

Now I want to go on a bit of a digression from finance theory to understand how it applies to your own specific situation. We said that we want to maintain purchasing power over time, but your purchasing basket doesn't necessarily track the average inflation rate. So whether you're saving for your kid's education or a vacation home in the south of France, you want your assets to grow in such a way that you're on the way to achieving your own targets.

It's important to note, and I can't state this enough, that your own targets have nothing to do with what the stock market averages are doing. Trying to keep up with a persistently buoyant market is a dangerous game to play if you don't need those types of returns to achieve your goals.

Maybe we can then define risk as the possibility that you won't reach your goals.

Yep, that's it. That's the definition of risk that really matters to you.

Now I'm going to tell you something that might surprise you.

The vast majority of money invested in the markets has a completely different definition of risk.

Instead, these large investors define risk as deviating from the returns generated by broad market benchmarks.

Wait ... what?

So let me get this straight—if the market is down 10 percent next year, these investors define risk as *not* losing 10 percent next year?

Pretty much!

Institutional managers, who represent the vast majority of money invested in the stock market, obsess over metrics like "tracking error" (basically, how different your performance is from the broad market benchmark) and "information ratio" (an odd and silly measurement that is higher—and interpreted as better—the closer you can keep to the broad market's performance).

And on a practical basis, the guys actually managing the money define their own personal risk as the risk of getting fired. They don't need to worry about protecting your money or preserving your purchasing power. They don't know you and will never meet you. If the market is down 10 percent, they'll get a pat on the back for only being down 8 percent. They just don't want to be down 12 percent. And so low-risk investing to them is tracking the benchmark as closely as possible—but not going under. It's like a bizarro version of *The Price Is Right*.

If you're new to the market and confused after reading this, that's good. It means you have common sense, and you haven't yet been corrupted by academic finance theory. There is hope for you yet!

Academic finance looks at your stock portfolio and sees "asset class exposure" designed to earn an "equity risk premium" over time. It tells you to own as many different stocks as possible in order to eliminate "non-systematic risk" from your portfolio, leaving only "systematic risk" and giving you access to stock market "beta."

Huh?

To academic finance, losing money isn't "risk," it's part of the game. Instead, they see "risk" as not getting access to all that juicy "beta."

This is, of course, nonsense.

When you talk about the risk to your savings, you're talking about losing money. And, more accurately, you should be talking about losing purchasing power.

Financial writer Jason Zweig wrote a column for *Money* magazine way back in the go-go days of January 2000, when the market was soaring and it seemed that everyone was becoming a stock market millionaire. He interviewed dozens of residents of Boca Raton, Florida, asking if their portfolios had beaten the market. Some said yes, and some said no, but the most memorable quote he pulled for the article was from one man who said, "Who cares? All I know is, my investments earned enough for me to end up in Boca."

And that pretty much sums it up. Why worry what everyone else is doing when you're in Boca?

Once again, two groups who need to communicate, investors and money managers, are not speaking the same language. All this talk about "risk" is really just us talking over each other. Which is incredibly dangerous, because when all is said and done, the only thing you have control over when constructing your portfolio is your risk exposure.

17

UNDERSTAND WHY
LOW RISK RULES

---

*To enjoy a reasonable chance for continued better than average
results, the investor must follow policies which are (1) inherently
sound and promising, and (2) not popular on Wall Street.*

BENJAMIN GRAHAM

A surprising truth

You know that you should get paid to take risk—I've already
told you that. And anyone with a passing knowledge of investing knows that risk and return are joined at the hip. More risk
equals more potential return. Everybody knows this!

So if you own a large basket of risky penny stocks, will that
outperform a basket of safe low-risk blue chips?

Nope. It almost certainly will not.

You must insist on getting paid to assume risk. But you can't
assume that taking risk will get you paid.

In fact, research across time periods and global markets
has proven that you will earn a higher return in low-risk stocks

than you will in high-risk stocks. And you will earn this higher return with lower portfolio volatility.

This is what's known as the low-risk anomaly. And it turns everything we think we know about investing on its head.

For an opportunity that flies so low under the radar, it's surprising to learn that the low-risk anomaly has been covered in several academic studies going all the way back to the early 1970s. It has been tested and re-tested over the years, mostly because there is universal agreement that *it doesn't make any sense that this anomaly exists.*

Much of the research on the anomaly has focused on trying to understand *why* it works, because there is incontrovertible evidence that it *does* work. It seems to offer the proverbial free lunch, so researchers cast a skeptical eye on it. What causes it? Is it just a coincidence—that is, are there other factors that somehow explain it?

I'm going to try not to get too geeky in this section but there will be Greek letters, and for that I apologize in advance.

Most of the research defines what I refer to as "low risk" in one of two ways. First, there is "low beta," which is a relative measure. Low beta stocks are those that are relatively less volatile than the overall market. Then there is "low volatility," which is an absolute measure—stock prices that don't move around all that much. Recalling your high school statistics class, these are stock prices that demonstrate low standard deviation. Don't worry too much about the distinction, though. Whether you're talking about "low beta" or "low volatility," these are generally the same stocks (and they're not the ones most people are talking about, or that most investors are chasing).

The story begins in 1972, when Black, Jensen, and Scholes published a historic paper testing the Capital Asset Pricing Model (CAPM). The CAPM basically states that an asset's expected return is a combination of the risk-free rate and a risk premium, and it's a fundamental model upon which the theory of efficient markets rests. The paper's authors, however, were probably surprised to discover that "high-beta assets tend to have negative alphas, and low-beta assets tend to have positive alphas."

Translated into English, this means that investors were not being well compensated for taking risk. In fact, the opposite was true—"alpha," or investment outperformance, was more prevalent in lower-risk assets.

Right off the bat, this is a groundbreaking observation, albeit a bit inconvenient for the establishment, since by this point finance students were being taught that the risk line sloped up and to the right—more risk equals more return.

And in a 1972 working paper, Haugen and Heins concluded that, "after observing the performance of an extremely large number of issues over long periods of time, we find little support for the notion that risk premiums have, in fact, manifested themselves in realized rates of return."

That's a pretty blunt way of saying you don't get paid to take risk. Think about the implications that has for all of finance.

The problem is, the conclusion stood directly in opposition to academic finance orthodoxy. It made a mess of the formulas and graphs, and the neat conclusions offered by the CAPM. And it would have relegated many finance textbooks to the trash heap. That's not ideal, because textbooks are really expensive. It was hard for academic finance to say exactly what to do with this. And so most of the subsequent research attempts to verify this conclusion, to make sense of it, and to understand if it's an enduring anomaly or just a quirk of the data.

Skipping forward to 1992, finance legends Fama and French wrote a landmark paper titled "The Cross-Section of Expected Stock Returns," and while it focuses primarily on why smaller and cheaper stocks tend to outperform, it also mentions the surprising outperformance of low-beta stocks, stating that the theoretical market lines "underestimate the average returns on low-beta stocks and overestimate the average returns on high beta stocks."

Translation: we don't get paid as much to take risk as we think we do.

In 2010, Baker, Bradley, and Wurgler noted that between 1968 and 2008, "low-volatility and low-beta portfolios offered an enviable combination of high average returns and small drawdowns." The results were resounding: "Regardless of whether we define risk as volatility or beta or whether we consider all stocks or only large caps, low risk consistently outperformed high risk over the period."

It's a puzzle that they admit makes no sense. They note that it's compounded by the fact that:

- The lower-risk portfolio produced smoother returns and an easier ride up for investors

- Transaction costs were lower for the low-risk portfolios

The authors state: "These results are not new, but they have not been sufficiently emphasized, explained, or exploited."

Baker and Haugen did not hedge when titling their 2012 paper "Low Risk Stocks Outperform Within All Observable Markets of the World." Covering twenty-one years of data in twenty-one developed countries and twelve emerging markets, they present "compelling evidence for the anomaly." And they don't bury the lede, with the following opening paragraph:

> The fact that low risk stocks have higher expected returns is a remarkable anomaly in the field of finance. It is remarkable because it is persistent—existing now and as far back in time as we can see. It is also remarkable because it is

comprehensive. We shall show here that it extends to all equity markets in the world. And finally, it is remarkable because it contradicts the very core of finance: that risk bearing can be expected to produce a reward.

The conclusion is similarly blunt:

> As a result of mounting evidence presented by us and many serious practitioners, the basic pillar of finance, that greater risk can be expected to produce a greater reward, has fallen. It is now clear to a greater and greater number of researchers and practitioners that inside all of the stock (and even some bond) markets of the world the reward for bearing risk is negative. Greater risk, greater reward is a basic tenant of finance; thus its invalidation carries critical implications for the theories underlying investment and corporate finance. In our view, existing textbooks on both subjects are dramatically wrong and need to be rewritten.

Holy shit!

And then they take a side swipe at indexing:

> In terms of the investment theory, it is clear that the directive to invest in capitalization-weighted portfolios as a core strategy is ill-advised.

It goes on. The analysis and conclusions are clear and understandable to most. If you're interested in learning more about this, I advise you to seek it out.

But wait, there's still more. In their 2014 low-risk opus, titled "Betting Against Beta," Frazzini and Pedersen confirmed that high-beta investments deliver lower alpha—not just in the US stock market but also among "twenty international equity markets, Treasury bonds, corporate bonds, and futures."

In a 2014 paper, Baker, Bradley, and Taliaferro run the numbers on US stocks going back to 1968 and find that a dollar invested in the lowest-risk portfolio turned into $81.66, while a dollar in the highest-risk portfolio grew to only $9.76. Duplicating this in other global developed markets back to 1989 showed a low-risk advantage of $7.23 to $1.20.

Let me wrap up with a look at the work of van Vliet and Blitz. Together, they authored two papers: "The Volatility Effect: Lower Risk Without Lower Return" (2007) and "The Volatility Effect Revisited" (2019). Van Vliet puts the anomaly to work, managing a low volatility equity portfolio, and has also authored the book *High Returns from Low Risk*.

Van Vliet's work is notable for demonstrating that the anomaly exists in major markets in the US, Europe, and Japan, as well as in emerging markets. He has also created a "conservative formula," which he uses to screen for the most "conservative" stocks. As of this writing, he maintains a website at paradoxinvesting.com, where he makes available all of his datasets going back to 1929. The numbers are compelling. If you graph the most conservative versus the riskiest baskets of stocks since inception, you can barely see the high-risk line—it is absolutely dwarfed by the gains experienced by the conservative portfolio.

To be fair, some research papers cast a more skeptical eye towards the anomaly. In his 2016 paper "Understanding Defensive Equity," Robert Novy-Marx finds that the deck is stacked against high volatility and high beta stocks, since they disproportionately include small, unprofitable growth companies, and explains that once those stocks are removed from the averages, the outperformance of a low-risk portfolio makes a lot more sense. And yet he does not deny the poor performance of those risky, small, unprofitable stocks.

Indeed, this seems to be the main argument of those who insist this isn't a viable anomaly at all. In an appendix to his 2016 book *Your Complete Guide to Factor-Based Investing*, passive investing champion Larry Swedroe writes that "the anomaly is much more about the underperformance of high-volatility (or high-beta) stocks and not so much about the outperformance of low-volatility (or low-beta) stocks."

And here's where I think the academics kind of lose the plot. The idea that a portfolio of low-risk stocks outperforms primarily due to the absence of shitty lottery stocks in no way negates the low-risk investing message. It just reinforces it.

I say that the key to weight loss is to eat healthy. You say no, the key to weight loss is to eliminate junk food. We are taking different logical paths to the same conclusion.

We can argue about it. Or you could just... Put. That. Donut. Down.

I'll let the academic finance nerds fight this one out, secure in the knowledge that low-risk portfolios have reliably outperformed.

This leaves only one question to answer: Will the low-risk anomaly continue to work in the future?

As I've shown, there's not much argument against the fact that the low-risk anomaly works. But if we can understand *why* it works, we can better understand whether we can expect it to continue to work in the future.

As a basic rule, once an anomaly is well known, anyone can exploit it. So if the research surrounding the low-risk anomaly is true, investors should be bidding up the prices of these low-risk stocks. And by doing so, they should essentially eliminate the anomaly (because higher prices today mean lower returns tomorrow).

The finance community has known about the low-risk anomaly since 1972, and yet it persists. Why does this make any sense?

I'm going to give you five reasons.

1. Because ... math

Investment returns follow a geometric path, not an arithmetic one. The order of returns matters. And volatility can rob you of compound returns.

Example: Assume the following sequence of annual returns: +5 percent, –30 percent, +25 percent, +5 percent.

Add these returns up and they total 5 percent.

So if you invested $100 on day one, you would have $105 at the end of the four years... right?

Wrong.

In fact, you would have $96.47.

Why is this?

Because in year two you didn't lose 30 percent of $100... you lost 30 percent of $105.

And in year three you didn't gain 25 percent of $100... you gained 25 percent of $73.50.

Volatility is a tax on your compound returns. Remember that Warren Buffett quote: "Rule number one: don't lose money; rule number two: don't forget rule number one." This is what he's talking about!

Of course, Buffett doesn't mean that you should never risk losing money—any profit-seeking endeavor entails that possibility. But he wants you to be aware of the impact of losses on your long-term compound returns.

In fact, as I described earlier, Buffett's extraordinary record comes from preserving capital on the way down, not from outperforming the market on the way up.

The first reason why you should try to create a low-risk portfolio is because, well, math.

2. Because we are greedy

If you swing for the fences every time you enter the batter's box, you'll likely have a horrible batting average.

If every play is a Hail Mary targeting the end zone, the vast majority of passes will fall incomplete.

If you shoot for the net each time you touch the puck, you're going to miss far more often than you connect.

The discipline it takes to win is a lot less fun.

Have you ever been to the track and put a few bucks on a horse? If you're like me and you know very little about navigating a racing form, you probably look for a long shot with a cool name and place your bet. What fun is it to gamble on the 3:5 favorite? Nope. Give me the 15:1 long shot. I want to win big.

As far back as 1949, in the *American Journal of Psychology*, Richard Griffith identified that bettors prefer long-shot horses, and that these bets, on average, pay a lot less than the favorites. Due to demand from gamblers, the long shots are more expensive than they should be!

This is how the track makes money, and it's how novice investors overbid for long shots, reducing their ultimate profit. And it's a universal thing—just as it has persisted over the years in all types of sports gambling, it persists in the stock market.

Once again, it's a topic that Prospect Theory has already covered. People love lottery tickets. In the study, the vast majority of people would prefer a 0.1 percent chance at $5,000 over a sure $5. (Conversely, and highlighting the irrationality, an even larger majority would rather pay $5 than have a 0.1 percent chance of losing $5,000.) Some have speculated that there's a value in *anticipating* the big payday, which we are willing to pay for. And so one can argue that the person who is paying more than they should for a lottery stock is behaving rationally in that they are paying up for entertainment.

But that's not a smart way to take risk. And you know this from your business experience—taking too many stupid risks will eventually ruin you. Investors bid up the price of lottery stocks beyond where they should be. They pay too much for small companies with cheap shares. Companies loaded with debt. Companies in young industries with a wide range of potential outcomes. Companies with tremendous growth prospects and no profits to speak of (maybe even no revenues). And because investors bid up the price of these companies while ignoring the stodgy, boring, lower-risk stocks, the prospective return on the lower-risk stocks is actually higher than the higher-risk stocks.

Keep in mind that what I'm talking about here is returns on average. Yes, you might actually hit that lottery stock, and you'll make a lot more money in it than you would have in Walmart shares. But, on average, you are better off investing in Walmart.

If we can earn higher returns with lower risk, there is no rational reason to invest in higher-risk or higher-volatility stocks. In fact, investing in these shares is a highly irrational endeavor. Why would I ever take more risk in order to expect to earn a lower return?

And I will ask the question yet again: *Why doesn't everybody know about this?*

One reason might be because it eliminates a large part of what draws the average person to investing in the first place— the desire to "get rich." In the late '90s Nasdaq bubble, this was illustrated by the frenzy that existed around gambling in high-volatility technology stocks, particularly internet-related names. Literally everyone was playing the game, and many of us were making far more money trading stocks than we were in our day jobs. I knew several people who gave up the rat race entirely to trade stocks in their pajamas. The business was so popular that E-Trade ads became ubiquitous—and more than two decades later, we still recall the one with the patient being wheeled into the operating room because he had "money coming out the wazoo."

Investing becomes increasingly popular after a long market advance. Most people are drawn to equity markets near market tops, times at which investing in risky stocks has been working. So there aren't a lot of receptive ears for the message that risky stocks have a lower expected return. When you're near the top of the market, recent evidence just doesn't support it. Besides, everyone is here to get rich quick, not to wait for profits to compound over decades.

Sure, you can hit a lottery ticket stock and make a lot of money, but what if I told you that your long-term odds of success are better by buying mature, boring companies? Not as great a sales pitch, is it?

Human nature wins out. The reason we keep buying high-risk stocks is the reason we fall for fad diets and click on articles promising washboard abs in thirty days.

Nobody wants to hear that several years of consistent workouts and a calorie deficit is what you need to get back to the body of your glory days. And nobody wants to hear that buying boring, low-volatility stocks will ultimately be more profitable than having a basket of lottery ticket stocks. But both are true.

And so it ever will be.

I recall sitting down to review a portfolio with a client many years ago. He looked it up and down and said, "This is boring. You aren't any fun at all." I smiled and replied, "That's the point!"

3. Because we are horrible decision makers

Aside from the various ways we fool ourselves into paying too much for long-shot stocks, we are susceptible to many other biases that negatively impact our decision-making:

- Attention-grabbing bias—we gravitate to the flashiest stocks. The ones making headlines. The ones everyone is talking about. They tend to be the newest, most cutting-edge companies. And with so much of their value reliant on the distant future, they are also the most volatile.

- Representativeness bias—we look at a stock that has been a great performer and identify all of the similarities with the hot new stock we want to buy. We don't take an unbiased, critical view of it as an investment; we see only what we want to see. If you've ever bought a promising young company that you think will be "The Next (Insert Successful Company Name Here)," you have likely succumbed to this bias.

- Overconfidence—this is a big one for entrepreneurs, but we all suffer from it. Especially in the investment world, over-confidence in the face of disconfirming evidence is deadly.

This is but a sample of the biases that drive us into higher-risk, higher-octane stocks.

4. Because the incentives are all wrong

You would think that professional money managers, who by and large are aware of the research and the implications it holds for building portfolios, would apply more cold logic to the process than the average investor.

You would be wrong.

The professionals managing the big-money portfolios generally have one primary concern: to not get fired. And you do that by not trailing the market averages. Over short periods of time, it can be hard to do that with low-volatility stocks, particularly in rising markets (and markets are usually rising). Managers will tend to chase momentum stocks in order to produce the short-term track record upon which their current year bonus may be based.

5. Because there are constraints on rational managers

As most money in equity markets is managed through long-only strategies, there are restrictions around short selling. And so the price of the highest-volatility stocks will tend to be set by their most strident supporters. Without a check on that value, only the most bullish buyers are setting the price. And as the sellers step aside, the price will eventually reflect a huge amount of excess optimism.

And so, for these and various other reasons, it's a good bet to expect the low-risk anomaly to persist.

"The biggest risk is not taking one"

A reliable, low-risk way to outperform most investors, and to make the process of investing far less stressful? Yes, it exists. And the reasons that most people won't commit to it are the same reasons it will continue to work.

There's a way to steal returns from the market without paying the cost of increased risk. It's all about taking the right kind of risk.

Investing defensively actually puts the odds on your side, but low risk doesn't mean *no* risk. No matter how safe an investment might seem on the surface, there is no such thing as an investment that bears zero risk.

Even parking savings in a bank account entails risk. And I'm not talking about the long-shot risk of a potential bank failure, but the very real risk that your money will lose purchasing power while it sits "safely" in a bank account. Mellody

Hobson, president of Ariel Investments, says it best: "The biggest risk is not taking one."

There is literally nowhere to hide from risk.

Let's consider the humble bond. Bonds, in general, are not great investments. Bonds, at this specific point in time, suck.

The problem with bonds is that your upside is limited to the interest coupon. You're never going to be pleasantly surprised by an investment in a bond. You either get exactly what you signed up for, or you get disappointed. I suppose that's the price you pay for safety, but the safety itself is an illusion, particularly in periods of high inflation.

The key is to understand the difference between nominal and real returns.

You have a bond that pays 5 percent. That's your *nominal* return.

Inflation during the period is 3 percent. So your *real* return is 2 percent (5 percent minus 3 percent).

You pay tax at 50 percent. So your after-tax bond coupon is 2.5 percent (half of 5 percent). Inflation was 3 percent, so your effective *real* after-tax return is *minus* 0.5 percent.

Some bond issues, like US municipal bonds, offer investors tax-free interest coupons. This is better, but the coupon rate on these will generally be lower, to reflect the tax-free nature of the interest receipts. Better, but still not great.

So yep, bonds suck. Unless your real return is high enough to compensate for your tax expense, bonds guarantee you a very low return—maybe even a negative return. This is not the cornerstone of a low-risk investment strategy. Indeed, if we define risk as losing purchasing power over time, it's a strategy that almost ensures failure. The only way you possibly win is if inflation is lower than expected.

Having said this, bonds are a necessary evil. They can be a stabilizing force in your portfolio, because they tend to hold value, or even increase in value, at times of market stress.

So while bonds suck, if you choose not to hold any, you will end up increasing the risk and volatility in your overall holdings.

What we need to do is build a portfolio that gives you just enough risk to get you where you want to go. Not too little. Not too much. We want to dial in that risk just right.

Your goal should be to build a portfolio that allows you to hold less of your assets in bonds while still minimizing volatility.

Building a more conservative equity portfolio allows you to do this. We're going to focus on buying the kind of businesses you'd love to own. These businesses tend to have less volatile stock prices and therefore benefit from the low-risk anomaly. Developing an understanding of which strategies work and which don't will help you filter the noise and gain confidence in what your own advisor is doing for you.

18

INVEST, DON'T SPECULATE

In the short run, the market is a voting machine but in the long run, it is a weighing machine.

BENJAMIN GRAHAM

Speculating versus investing

The point of investing is to buy an asset for less than it's worth.

The goal of speculating is to buy an asset without regard to its value, in the hopes that someone will pay you more for it at some point in the future.

Too many people confuse investing with speculating.

I don't blame you if you're one of them, because we are inundated with financial media that perpetuates this misunderstanding.

If you're reading a headline that says "Investors Sell Stocks on Interest Rate Fears," then you should be aware that most true investors would not be selling based on short-term concerns around interest rates. The people selling are more accurately called "speculators," and they don't care about the long-term value of a business—they are just in it for a quick trade.

The first rule in filtering the financial news is to translate "investor" to "speculator" when required (and to be clear, this is most of the time).

Then remember that you're an investor, not a speculator. And then remember that speculators are playing a different game than you are. All of a sudden, that scary headline becomes a lot less scary. Speculators are selling? Good for them. I don't care. I'm not playing that game.

Let me put it to you bluntly—you should be investing, not speculating. But, unfortunately, many speculators are out there masquerading as investors. They might even be your investment advisors. If they're just regurgitating corporate information from CNBC or relying on pie-in-the-sky projections from overoptimistic management teams, they're likely just speculators.

Want to speculate? Gambling on sports or at the tables in Vegas is much more fun. The great thing about casinos is that they are very good at looking after their best customers. Comped meals and luxury suites, exclusive concert tickets, maybe even some "companionship" while you're in town.

Gamble there—not in the market.

The market will never comp you free tickets to Cirque du Soleil.

Choose the narrow path

There are companies with a narrow range of potential outcomes, and those with a wide range of outcomes. If your goal is to protect wealth rather than build it, you should prefer companies that have a narrow path ahead of them.

The following figures demonstrate two extreme examples. One is a lower-risk company—mature, with a nice defensible moat around its business, and a predictable path to sustained profitability. It likely won't make you rich, but it won't ruin you, either. You'll notice that the range of future outcomes is quite narrow.

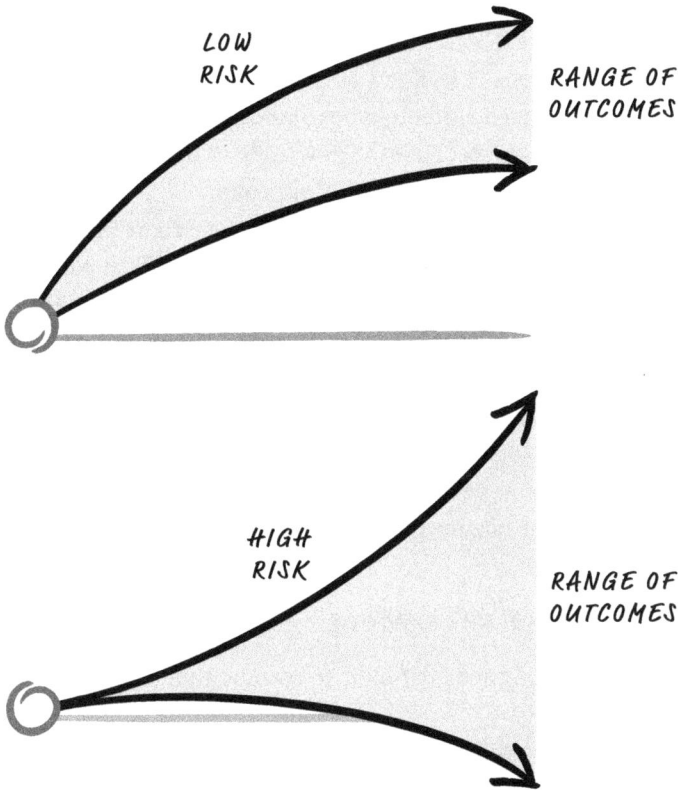

LOW RISK — RANGE OF OUTCOMES

HIGH RISK — RANGE OF OUTCOMES

The second figure is a high-risk company. It could make you rich. Or it could be a zero. The range is huge, and the further out you go, the less confidence there is in the business.

In life, the entrepreneur chooses the wide path. There is infinite possibility. But also no safety net. We would call this a life well lived, and a path that allows your unique skills to flourish.

Most people who build significant wealth do it via the wide path.

But when you're investing to protect your wealth, the wide path can lead to ruin.

Protecting wealth requires you to choose the narrow path. There is no need to chase the upside at this point. Protect your downside. Narrow your range of outcomes. Strive for predictability in the cash flows of the businesses you own. This will make it much easier for you to strengthen your conviction in your strategy—because the downside of the narrow path is higher than the downside of the wide path.

In order to protect your wealth, you must secure the floor of your net worth—don't worry about the ceiling. That will take care of itself, as long as you're invested in productive assets that can grow cash flows over time.

By managing the downside and protecting the floor, you won't be as likely to panic, and you won't be as likely to be shaken from your long-term strategy at the wrong time.

Invest, don't speculate.

Choose the narrow path.

Every market call is wrong

Part of avoiding speculation is to assume that all investment tips are wrong.

The worst thing you can do is buy or sell something because of a sound bite you heard on CNBC or read online. In investing, it's a recipe for disaster. Because even if the call works out for the person you heard it from, it might not work out at all for you.

First of all, you can't trust anything that you hear. Fund Manager A might be on CNBC touting a stock position. But let's be clear about something—Fund Manager A doesn't give a crap about your portfolio. You might think that Fund Manager A doesn't want to look like a fool on national TV, and so she's surely going to offer up one of her best ideas, right? Wrong. Fund Manager A cares about one thing and one thing only: making money for her investors, and therefore for herself. And if she's on CNBC touting a stock, there's a better than 50/50 chance that while you are rushing to your broker to buy shares, she's the one selling them to you.

Think that's unfair? So sorry. This is the way the game is played. It's vicious.

The market is dynamic—new facts arise daily, and investors change their minds as new evidence appears. And they won't go back on TV to tell you. There's a good chance that Fund Manager B no longer owns the hot stock he was pumping a few months ago, which is now down over 50 percent. But you're still in it, because you bought it on a whim and don't want to take the loss. He is under no obligation to go back on TV to tell you that he sold, and even if he did, you might have been watching a *Seinfeld* rerun that day and missed it.

For safety and sanity's sake, just assume that every investment tip you receive is wrong.

Potato chips and penny stocks

One small bet on a speculative stock isn't so bad, right?

I've seen all sorts of "next big things" over the years—before I knew better, many of them were in my own portfolio! Early stage biotech. Junior gold miners. Fledgling software companies. Near-bankrupt retailers primed for a turnaround. Revolutionary medical equipment manufacturers. The list goes on and on. The most speculative of them are often called penny stocks, but they can be priced far higher than a dollar. The principle is the same. I've seen these companies trading for hundreds of dollars per share and still retain the spirit of the penny stock.

Low stock prices seem to draw people. As the thinking goes, it's easier for a 10-cent stock to go to a dollar than it is for a 10-dollar stock to go to a hundred.

No matter what the market price of the stock, if there's one thing all of these companies have in common, it's a dream of multiplying your money several times over via a great story, a promotional management team, and promises of vast riches.

Let's call them "lottery stocks." They're close cousins to the venture capital lottery tickets we talked about earlier—the promise is that this one investment could change your life.

But historical evidence tells us that these high-risk gambles, on average, don't pay off. There's no definitive reason for this to be the case, but my own theory is that the lottery ticket aspect of these stocks makes them extraordinarily attractive to speculators, which means their value gets bid up higher than it should. For some reason, this is often worse with the lowest-priced stocks. (And if you doubt this, ask yourself if you would stop yourself from buying a stock if it cost you 11 cents a share instead of 10 cents a share, and then ask yourself if you would do the same for a stock that was $110 versus $100. We rationalize away the cent as meaningless, even though the difference in both cases is a 10 percent premium.)

So let's say you're behaving yourself, holding a portfolio that is 98 percent made up of intelligent, blue-chip, quality companies. You'd like to gamble with that last 2 percent.

And I won't stop you. I've done the same. But before you go ahead with it, consider the potato chip.

When's the last time you had just one?

You see, the lottery stock purchase is a lot like a slot machine. Have you ever seen anyone pull once and walk away?

So let's play out a couple of possible scenarios.

You could bet on the lottery stock and lose. You told yourself you would just walk away. But that doesn't happen. Prospect theory tells us that "a person who has not made peace with his losses is likely to accept gambles that would be unacceptable to him otherwise." So after experiencing a loss, we are more likely to take on another large risk in order to recover that loss. Many of us know a person who has gone on tilt, emptying their bank account in a disastrous casino adventure. Some of us have even been that person. This phenomenon explains it.

On the other hand, you could bet on that lottery stock and win. In this case, overconfidence bias takes over. You're more inclined to take on that risk again. You might begin to think that the lottery stock game is easy, or that you have some sort of system or specific insight that works. The technical term for this is "dumb luck," and while I'll certainly take it, I wouldn't bet that it will continue in the future. Over time you are likely to give back all of your winnings.

Another possible outcome is that the stock does nothing. It might vacillate between 5 and 15 cents for years. It might occasionally pop to 30 or 40 cents—and you won't sell, of course, because you think it could be the start of a huge move ... until it drops back down to 10 cents. As the lottery stock languishes, you grow bored of the story, and years later just sell the damn thing to get it out of your portfolio. If you're lucky, you'll break even on it. It wasn't worth the opportunity cost of the money invested in it, or the time and mental bandwidth you wasted on it.

And what makes me an expert on lottery stocks? I've done everything I've just described. Been there, done that. Experienced the overconfidence, the disappointment, and the boredom. Over the years the only people I've seen reliably get rich off of these stocks are the ones issuing shares to themselves and selling them to people like you and me. It's a shady group of characters you wouldn't trust to return your pen after you lent it to them, let alone manage a company you own a piece of.

Once again, our behavioral foibles work against our best interests. If you're trying to eat healthy, don't fool yourself into thinking you can have just one or two potato chips. And if you're trying to invest intelligently, do your best to resist the call of the lottery stock.

Prepare to be tested

Remember that the stock market was built for traders. It allows you to trade in and out of positions in seconds, moving money around at the speed of light.

But you're not going to use the stock market for trading.

You're going to do better than the vast majority of speculators, but this is going to require you to ignore certain "features" the market grants you, like the ability to trade constantly.

But, inevitably, you will be tested.

Your brother-in-law will have a hot tip on a penny stock.

Your moron neighbor will hit it big on a tiny biotech play.

You'll be compelled to buy shares in "the next big thing" after reading a random article on a random website.

I can almost guarantee this will happen.

Just remember that you are here to invest, not to speculate.

Speculating cash should come out of the same basket that funds your trips to Vegas, or your annual Super Bowl wager. Not out of your investment portfolio. If you must, carve out a (very) small slice of your portfolio to seed a "play" account, and don't mingle this with your empire of long-term business holdings.

Wealth preservation demands that you invest. Don't speculate.

HONOR YOUR INVESTMENT EDGE

The stock market is a wonderfully efficient mechanism for transferring wealth from the impatient to the patient.

WARREN BUFFETT

Your one edge

Years ago, when my job involved selecting investment managers for my clients' portfolios (yep, I was also once an allocator), one of the questions I would ask every manager was "What is your edge?"

The big money managers have all of the PhDs and global analyst teams. They are fully stocked with all sorts of proprietary analytics. They pay for exclusive information designed to give them insights into what's going on in the economy and the industries they cover. But most of them have performance that hovers around the averages.

Why is this?

An investing edge is ephemeral. One day it's there, the next day it's gone. Once a certain investment style has made a lot of money, it attracts more practitioners. The more people who are out there pursuing a strategy, the more it works ... until it doesn't. At a certain point, everyone who is going to implement the strategy has already done so. And with no new money coming in, the only direction for prices to go is down. It is extraordinarily difficult to sustain outperformance based on a perceived investment edge.

So what's your edge?

I'm about to reveal it to you—and it's not based on any complicated formulas or proprietary data. It's easy to understand and will persist over time.

Your edge is that you don't care how your portfolio does in the near term.

Well ... you *shouldn't* care how it does in the near term.

And so if you *do* care what it's doing today, this week, this month, or this quarter, then you're giving up your one and only edge over the pros.

To illustrate, I'll explain to you how most big money is invested. It is "overseen" by a board or committee, which receives a quarterly report from a consultant. These consultants comb over the decisions of portfolio managers in the context of explaining why each segment of the portfolio performed as it did relative to its benchmark in the past quarter.

There's nothing magical about the calendar quarter, but these arbitrary beginning and endpoints become the focus of the committee's analysis. The consultant will explain which stocks or sectors each manager should have owned, or which ones they should have avoided, in order to have performed better. One quarter the portfolio manager will be praised for owning a company, and the next quarter they will be criticized for it. It all depends on what "the market" decided to do during this past arbitrary three-month period.

Money managers playing this game can feel like a dog chasing its own tail. Obsessing over short-term performance is a losing game, and yet consultants and boards continue this pattern, if only out of habit, reinforcing the same tendency.

What's at stake for the portfolio managers in this game is nothing less than their livelihood. If a particular firm under-performs for long enough, consultants will recommend that clients pull their money out. If enough clients depart, it will impact the portfolio manager's bonus, and eventually job security. And so, due to these incentives, a myopic fixation on short-term performance is endemic in the investment indus-try. Remember—even God would probably get fired!

Nitpicking portfolio performance each and every quarter is a horrible way to invest. But it's what most of the big money out there is doing.

So the way the investment managers deal with this is to give the consultants what they want. If 5 percent of the bench-mark is a piece-of-shit, overpriced stock, the manager will express their displeasure by only allocating 4 percent of your portfolio to that piece of shit. Sounds nuts, but if that particu-lar stock has been going up recently, the manager would prefer to have some allocation to it in order to avoid the indignity of an extended period of underperformance.

Yes, it's stupid. We know it's stupid. Many investment firms simply refuse to play this game, at the cost of disqualifying themselves from the institutional allocator beauty pageant.

Your edge, investing your own capital, is that you can refuse to play it as well.

You can invest in stories that evolve over years, not months or quarters. Consequently, the game actually becomes easier to play.

Tracking every small short-term movement in the stocks you own works against you and serves to dull your investment edge.

Hiring a consultant or allocator to watch over the minutiae of the trades of your managers and reporting back to you every quarter will give you a sense that someone is "watching over" your money, but in the long run it won't add even a bit to your long-term returns. In fact, it's likely to do the opposite.

Your investment edge over the professionals and institutions is that you can afford to ignore the short term. You don't care if you underperform a benchmark index for a while, as long as you preserve capital. So while others avoid out-of-favor companies and industries, you can accumulate shares with patience, knowing that it will eventually pay off. While everyone else is fretting over the headlines and worried about this quarter's earnings, you're looking several years down the road. Keep your eyes on the horizon and you'll find that you've got an edge over even the largest and most well-resourced investors.

Maintain your long time horizon

If you want to have a durable investment edge, you have to maintain a long time horizon. This is easy to do when markets are tranquil and rising, but can be far more difficult when the news is at its worst. When things are bad, we tend to shorten our time horizons.

Normally, when the economy and stock market are doing well, investors are willing to pay a high price for future earnings. They might be willing to pay a lot for a company that has no current income, on the assumption that in a few years the profits will start rolling in. In this scenario, comfortable in their long-term assessment of the company, it's easy for them to ignore short-term bad news.

But when things don't look great, investor time horizons compress. All of a sudden they become unusually concerned with what will happen this quarter, this month, or even this week.

They hang on every word management utters in a conference call. They extrapolate bad news reported by a competitor to the entire industry. And they scour the news for reasons to sell.

As you can imagine, this is a time when prices become volatile, and when most investors overreact to bad news. They suddenly forget that the vast majority of a company's value comes from earnings that will come well into the future, long after the current troubles are forgotten.

The successful investor must maintain this long time horizon. Times when everyone else has extreme myopia offer the greatest rewards to farsighted investors who remember that all periods of trouble eventually pass.

And yet so many investors, especially those new to having significant assets in the stock market, feel like they need to anticipate the next market correction, take profits off the table, and go to cash. This is almost always a horrible idea. In the oft-quoted words of legendary fund manager Peter Lynch, "Far more money has been lost by investors preparing for corrections, or trying to anticipate corrections, than has been lost in corrections themselves."

The entrepreneur should be uniquely positioned to maintain this understanding. You have learned over the years to take advantage of opportunities—using downturns to buy distressed assets out of receivership, acquire weaker competitors, or secure prime retail locations vacated by tenants. Having a long-term view is the way to emerge from downturns stronger than ever.

You wouldn't be where you are today if you listened to the Chicken Littles or panicked every time the economic outlook appeared grim. Take this essential element of success and apply it to your investment portfolio as well.

This is your only edge over the pros. Honor it.

20

EMBRACE BOREDOM

If investing is entertaining, if you're having fun, you're probably not making any money. Good investing is boring.

GEORGE SOROS

Chasing growth is hard

There is an ever-present temptation to buy shares in the most exciting, fastest-growing companies. Many novice investors assume that the only way to grow your portfolio is to buy shares in companies that are growing at high rates. The evidence, surprisingly, shows the opposite.

In the December 2019 *Journal of Finance* paper "Diagnostic Expectations and Stock Returns," researchers confirmed a 1996 analysis showing that "returns on portfolios of stocks with the most optimistic analyst long term earnings growth forecasts are substantially lower than those for stocks with the most pessimistic forecasts."

Huh?

You're telling me that the companies expected to grow earnings the most performed *worse* than companies with the most pessimistic earnings forecasts?

That's exactly what I'm telling you.

The paper is a dense one, with over fifty pages full of formulas and charts, but it is summarized neatly in the following chart, which is based on analyst estimates and market data collected by the researchers between 1981 and 2015. The universe of stocks is segregated into deciles, with the lowest projected earnings growth rates on the left, and the highest on the right. The subsequent return is reflected in the bar length. Reliably, over time, the stocks that analysts believe will exhibit the strongest growth actually perform far worse than the stocks that have the lowest growth projections.

ANNUAL RETURNS FOR PORTFOLIOS FORMED ON LONG-TERM EARNINGS PER SHARE GROWTH FORECASTS

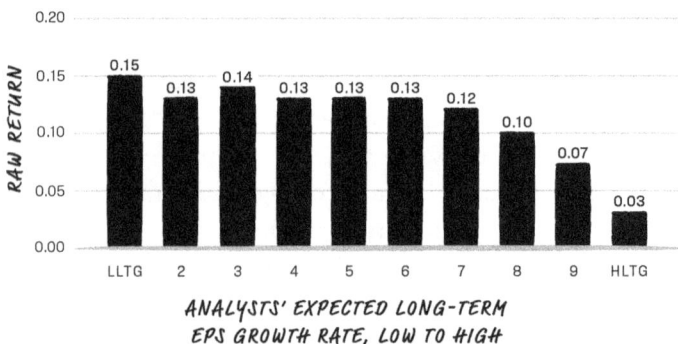

ANALYSTS' EXPECTED LONG-TERM EPS GROWTH RATE, LOW TO HIGH

To the non-professional investor, this makes no sense. You might be asking: "Isn't the whole idea of investing to grow your capital by identifying the fastest-growing companies?" You might think that searching for the next Google is the ideal way to build your portfolio, but as the researchers demonstrated, it's not.

Why is this? Well, a big reason is that higher-growth companies are more expensive than lower-growth companies.
This is because investors are anticipating this growth, and
therefore bidding up the prices of these companies. And so
for an investor to earn a premium return on their money, the
company needs to not only grow fast, but to *grow at a faster
rate than the market expects.*

And here's where things get difficult. The vast majority of
high-growth companies do not maintain their growth rates.
Portfolio manager Steven Romick highlights this by analyz-
ing data between 1979 and 2020. He takes the top 1,000 US
companies with over 10 percent earnings growth, and looks
at how many of them were able to maintain this growth over
subsequent years. Only 353 of those companies maintained a
10 percent growth rate in the subsequent year. After three
years, only seventy-four of the original 1,000 were left. And
after five years, only twenty-one remained. And because most
basic stock analysis seems to be nothing more than extrapolating recent growth into the future, most growth companies
will disappoint.

Chasing individual growth names is hard, but just as difficult
is the temptation to chase fads. The idea is the same—identify
an area of promising growth, and make some big bets on it.

The thing is, investors don't call them fads. They are
"theme investing strategies," "new paradigm" companies, or
"new economy" stocks. They are the companies of the future
operating in the industries of the future, and anyone casting a
skeptical eye on them is behind the times.

And unfortunately, as the exchange-traded fund (ETF)
and indexing industry has thrived, more and more products
are created that are intended to capitalize on these fads. Just
because a fund company creates an ETF for a new hot investment area, it doesn't serve as validation of that idea. It's just

a symptom of a business that will package and sell anything that people will buy.

In a 2021 research paper, Ben-David, Franzoni, Kim, and Moussawi track the performance of "specialized ETFs that track niche portfolios and charge high fees," concluding that "these products perform poorly as the hype around them vanishes, delivering negative risk-adjusted returns." Quantifying their analysis, they show that "specialized ETFs persistently generate negative alphas of about –3.1 percent per year."

Recall that "alpha" means investment outperformance versus your benchmark. So, yup, that means that these strategies, on average, underperform the broader market by over 3 percent per year. That's huge.

There are a couple of lessons here.

The obvious one is not to chase fads that promise extreme growth.

Less obvious is that, even though you own a portfolio of ETFs—which are widely seen as prudent, low-cost investment vehicles—that doesn't mean you have a prudent, well-diversified portfolio. Because ETFs are created to be sold, and high growth sells.

Before leaving this topic, I thought it would be fun to revisit some of the larger investor manias in recent history. You may have read about the tulip bubble of 1637, the South Sea bubble of 1720, and the 1840 frenzy around investing in railway stocks, but recent history suggests that a knowledge of history and a supercomputer in your pocket may not help you avoid the follies of the past—in fact, there's an argument that social media has thrown accelerant on the fire of bubble creation.

Here is a partial list of some recent speculative frenzies and the approximate years of each. Be honest. How many of these did you take part in?

- Nifty Fifty stocks (1967–1972)
- Japanese real estate (1980s)
- Tech/telecom (1996–2000)
- Oil (2008)
- Housing (2008)
- Rare earth metals (2010)
- Fracking (2011)
- Biotech (2012–2015)
- 3D printing (2014)
- Marijuana (2018–2019)
- Crypto/NFTS (2021)

There will always be a hot new investment fad. A new paradigm. And those of us who cast a skeptical eye will be seen as hopelessly behind the times. But even when the predictions are correct, there's no guarantee that investors will make money.

Chasing growth is hard, and you should try to resist the urge to do so.

Because there is a much better way.

Defense wins championships

In the late '90s, while the whole world was on offense, seemingly getting rich on the promise of this amazing new thing called the "internet," I debated a friend of mine who refused to play the growth stock game. Steady and stoic, he invested defensively in Canadian bank stocks. "Bank stocks never go down for long," he told me. I mocked his conservatism in what I perceived as stocks more well suited for a retiree's account. "You go ahead and wait for your measly little dividends," I told him, "while I get rich."

History, of course, has been very kind to the Canadian banks— a government-protected oligopoly that has just become more entrenched into the economic fabric over time. And not so kind to the internet stocks of the 1990s.

So I became curious. What if, instead of chasing internet stocks back in the 1990s, one had just stuck to this boring approach that the younger me looked down upon?

I ran some numbers—keeping it simple with two very high profile and successful companies.

In the low-risk corner: Toronto Dominion Bank (now known as TD Bank)—a Canadian banking powerhouse that also built a strong US presence with retail branches and discount brokerage.

In the growth corner: Cisco Systems. One of the hottest stocks of the 1990s, and the most valuable company in the world for a brief period of time. It would have been too easy to pit TD Bank against Pets.com, so let's go with Cisco. An undeniably great company, Cisco is still around (and thriving!) today.

LAST PRICE   CSCO   TD

Source: Bloomberg

I started keeping track in mid-1996, just as the internet bubble really began to pick up steam. This allows us to take fully into account Cisco's meteoric rise. As you can see in the chart above, in early 2000 the investment in Cisco would have been about 8x as valuable as your investment in the boring, old, lumbering TD Bank.

However, the subsequent crash wasn't kind to Cisco at all. It was dead money for a decade, only starting to recover well into the middle of the 2010s. Meanwhile, like the tortoise to Cisco's hare, TD Bank plodded along and, except for a scary episode in the 2008/09 global banking crisis, has generally outperformed the faster grower.

But here's the thing with that previous chart—it's not quite accurate. It completely ignores the dividends you would have earned on the TD shares. When we take those dividends into account, and reinvest them in TD shares, the picture looks very different.

TOTAL RETURN INDEX   ● CSCO
(INCLUDING DIVIDENDS)   ● TD

Source: Bloomberg

This isn't even close. Your investment in the "boring" bank stocks has outperformed the exciting, high-growth company by more than 2x, and it's done it with a lot less drama.

My friend who refused to take part in the internet stock craze, who I openly mocked, had the last laugh. He has experienced decades of steady growth in his portfolio of safe, dividend-paying stocks. Meanwhile, I spent far too much time in search of the next great growth company, completely ignoring these low-risk massive wealth-creation machines because I perceived them as "too boring."

Lest you think I'm cherry-picking, the reality is that I actually gave the growth stocks the benefit of the doubt here. I could have chosen any number of optical equipment makers who languished post-crash (the ones I happened to own), but instead I chose Cisco, a company that since the turn of the century has grown revenue at 4.9 percent per year and earnings at 8.5 percent annually for twenty years. That's a solid track record through several economic cycles, including a crash that laid waste to the industry that Cisco sat at the core of. The problem, and the reason for the underperformance of Cisco, is that because expectations were so high, the odds were stacked against anyone betting that growth would continue.

It took me a few market cycles to finally learn that the simple investment strategy I had written off as boring is actually far superior to more elaborate, exciting, and seemingly intelligent strategies.

Most amazing of all is that it's surprisingly easy to follow... as long as you don't let your biases and weakness get in the way of doing what's best. Always remember, as the old football saying goes, defense wins championships.

Finding "the next Amazon"

With the benefit of hindsight, we think we should have seen today's winners well in advance. But is that necessarily true?

Think of today's most dominant companies.

In retrospect, Apple seems like an inevitability. But it wasn't, even after the introduction of the iPhone. Blackberry was dominant. Palm before that. It was once just a company that made pastel-colored computers that didn't work with any of your software.

Facebook (now Meta) was just another social network, many of which had risen and fallen before it. It was supposed to die out once our parents became active on it, rendering it terminally uncool. The next MySpace? That was the assumption.

And then there's Amazon. There's an iconic photo that has lately made its way around the internet. Jeff Bezos, sitting on a tiny desk (legend has it made out of a door) in a cramped office, with a banner taped to the wall, spray painted with the name "amazon.com." Many of us are old enough to remember the early days of Amazon, a pioneering internet retailer, which sold books. Only books. The kind made of paper. You would order off their website and they would mail them to you. It was all very quaint.

We previously discussed the "what if" of investing in Amazon back in the 1990s.

Well, I was around back then, investing my own money, and I did not invest in Amazon. I did, however, invest in a company that I thought would become the next Amazon.

Even back then, Amazon was a hot stock, and a hot company. And in those days, the online retail business model was ripe for replication. The best way to do this in the early days of the internet (this was before WiFi and smartphones, and we were all on dialup internet connections) was to sell a standardized product. No trying things on, no wondering about the fabric or the fit or the color—just selling something predictable. And, of course, solving the "long tails" problem—I could find books on Amazon that my local bookstore didn't have the shelf space to stock.

A natural extension of this was music. CDs were next only to books in terms of being easy to sell online. (And if you're too young to know what a CD is, look it up. I'm not going to go through the indignity of explaining my old man technology to you.)

CDNow was created to fill this gap. Founded by two brothers in 1994, the same year that Bezos founded Amazon, at its peak in 1998 the company was valued at over $1 billion. Unlike Amazon, which sold stodgy books to an older demographic, CDNow was appealing to a younger up-and-coming consumer group in new ways. One of the key differentiating advantages of its offering was the ability to sample every track on a disc before committing to buy it. For a music lover, it was awesome.

Like Amazon, CDNow was planting a flag on the internet, owning a category, and investing a boatload of cash in order to do so. Also just like Amazon, it was bleeding financially.

I owned a piece of CDNow, and when Amazon announced in 1998 that they were going to expand beyond books, there was some fear that they would begin competing with CDNow. But the winner was not a foregone conclusion—after all, there were loyal clients of both retailers, and there was no guarantee that Amazon would be able to gain a foothold in the music market.

It's not much of a spoiler to reveal that CDNow was not the next Amazon. In fact, after the market crashed in 2000, it was acquired for just over $100 million, netting the founding brothers a cool $17 million. Not bad, but a far cry from the billion-dollar valuation at the company's peak.

In a final indignity, the company's website became nothing more than a front for Amazon music sales, when the acquirer, Bertelsmann, slashed expenses to the bone and used Amazon for fulfillment of orders. By 2013, the brand was worthless and the URL disappeared.

In retrospect, we all knew Amazon would eat the world, right?

Except we didn't.

Your investment in the next hot stock might be the next Amazon. Or it might be just another CDNow. The hard thing about investing is that there is only one Amazon, but there are thousands of CDNows. And until the story plays itself out, there's no way to know which you own.

What this all means is that it's very difficult to search for extra returns in high-growth areas (or emerging markets, or exotic alternatives). An easier option is to just let the managers of the public companies you own allocate capital on your behalf.

You might think you're missing out, but you've really just outsourced the decision-making to industry expert professionals. It's one less thing that can derail your investment plan, and one less thing to worry about.

Chasing growth is hard. The odds are stacked against you. And the returns show that it's not even worth the hassle. Let's keep it simple. Seek your entertainment elsewhere. Let your portfolio bore the crap out of you.

21

CONVICTION IS THE KEY

If you would not have a man flinch
when the crisis comes, train him before it comes.

SENECA

Premeditatio malorum

The ancient stoic philosophers introduced me to an idea they called "premeditatio malorum"—the premeditation of evils.

It's a practice that involves considering some of the worst things that can possibly happen to you, as a way of immunizing yourself against them. To many, this concept might seem somewhat odd and quite grim, but if the stoic philosophy appeals as much to you as it does to me, you can see the value in it.

In fact, the idea of premeditatio malorum is rooted in our religious and cultural traditions. From the ancient Bhutanese folk saying "to be a happy person, one must contemplate death five times daily" to the writings of St. John Climacus ("The remembrance of death, like all other blessings, is a gift of God"), spiritual wisdom reminds us to keep in our minds that our time on earth is temporary and fleeting.

Paradoxically, this practice can actually make us happier. Remembering that you could lose your job makes you appreciate those administrative tasks you can't stand.

Being thankful for your health and the use of your limbs makes it hard to complain about all that yard work you need to get done.

And recalling the mortality of your loved ones will have you treasuring every routine moment with them, and hugging them a little tighter.

It's a useful practice.

Now we're going to apply it to your investment portfolio.

You see, at the start of almost any financial advisory relationship, you will work through a questionnaire that outlines your attitude towards risk. "How would you react if your portfolio fell 20 percent?" is a common question, for example. And "I would hold on or buy more" is a common answer.

The thing is, you have no idea how you would react in that scenario, because it's presented in such an abstract and soulless way.

In more vivid and personal terms, one might phrase it as follows:

You have worked your whole life and have finally sold your business for $10 million, after tax. You are ecstatic but also worried about what the future holds. You've never had responsibility for so much wealth, and you're not sure if you're handling it correctly. You hire an advisor recommended by your brother-in-law because he seems knowledgeable. Shortly after he deploys your cash, the market begins to decline. Your $10 million is now $9.5 million. "Don't worry," says your brother-in-law's advisor, "this is a healthy correction." This does not feel healthy at all, but you assume he's an expert and you trust him. After a brief respite, the market suffers another violent selloff. The newspapers begin talking about a big recession... maybe even another Great Depression scenario.

The financial news is filled with talking heads in fancy suits telling you to raise cash and head for the hills. Your $10 million is now $8 million, only a few months after investing. At this rate, your life's work will be vaporized in a couple of years. You demand another meeting with your brother-in-law's advisor, who tells you, "This is a healthy correction," and offers to switch you into a lower-risk fund, maybe to rebalance into bonds. What do you do?

If your answer to this scenario is "hold on or buy more," you're a more trusting and patient client than I would ever be.

Premeditatio malorum is about anticipating these events in advance.

That's a nice portfolio you got there ... would you still feel as confident in it if it was down 20 percent tomorrow?

Why conviction is important

Having confidence in the assets you're invested in will go a long way in helping you overcome the behavioral investment traps described in Chapter 3. Because if you understand what you own, are prepared for what can go wrong, and know how you are going to deal with it, then you will have the tools to overcome the temptation to make emotional decisions on the fly.

Research firm Dalbar conducts a well-known survey that tracks the difference between market returns and those returns actually experienced by investors. The results are often striking. For example, in 2018 they noted that the average balanced fund portfolio returned 6.8 percent per year over the twenty-year period from 1998 to 2017. During the same period, the average investor in those same funds experienced a return of 2.6 percent.

How is that possible? Because investors buy when prices are high and the news is positive, and sell when prices are low and the news is negative. In doing so, they ensure they will earn poor returns.

Many advisors use this data to prove to clients that they should stop trying to time the markets and instead stick to their investment plan. This is true.

But what if part of the problem causing this was a mismatch between the investor and their portfolio?

What if part of the reason they were selling is because they never really believed in their investment strategy to begin with?

A well-known example is that of Ken Heebner's CGM Focus Fund, the best-performing mutual fund of the first decade of the 2000s. The ten-year annualized return was an impressive 18.2 percent. In 2007 alone, the fund was up 80 percent, attracting $2.6 billion of assets the following year.

And then . . . the housing crash. The mortgage and banking crisis. The Great Recession. Immediately following a huge inflow of investor dollars, the fund declined 48 percent.

The money came in when the numbers were hot. But the investors didn't have conviction in Heebner or his strategy. They were just chasing returns. And so despite the fund having the best returns of any fund in the decade, investors performed horribly. According to Morningstar, the average investor in CGM Focus experienced a *loss* of 11 percent annually over the same time period that the manager made 18 percent per year.

There is no better illustration of why it's important to avoid chasing returns. Know why you're making an investment. Understand the strategy and have conviction in it. Because if you're just chasing returns, you're going to bail when things get rough.

Premeditatio malorum is important because it's a way to test for conviction. And conviction is the key to investing successfully through downturns.

The long-term trend in the markets, as in the economy, is up. Believing this is a necessary prerequisite to investing in stocks.

We all know what we need to do when the market corrects. When we're facing a recession scenario, or a financial crisis. When everyone else is panicking and selling. We need to buy.

But human nature tells us that we'll feel so much more comfortable running with the herd. And if the herd is selling, we also want to sell.

We will sell, even though we know it's the wrong thing to do in the long run, because it will alleviate our pain in the short run.

So what do we need in order to prevent ourselves from selling at the bottom?

I'll take it a step further—what do we need in order to *buy more* at the bottom?

The magic ingredient is *conviction*.

Conviction means that you have a firm belief in what you own or in the strategy being implemented by your money manager.

It means that you won't be tempted to sell when the market drops temporarily, no matter how violent the selloff.

In fact, it means that when that happens, you'll actually be tempted to buy more.

I'm not talking about blind faith. I'm talking about having a solid understanding of what you own. Confidence backed by objective facts, not predictions of what other investors will do.

The downside of conviction

Professional investors know that they need to develop conviction in the individual companies they own. Because understanding what you own is the key to holding on when the price declines. It's the secret to buying when everyone else is selling. And it's the element that gives you the confidence to allocate a big chunk of your portfolio to your best ideas.

You can apply this same concept to your own portfolio—developing conviction in the managers you hire and the strategies they implement. The benefits of doing so are no less important.

But conviction can be a double-edged sword. While it's a necessary ingredient to staying the course when everyone around you is panicking, it can also mean that you're wrong and unwilling to accept any contrary information—firmly entrenching yourself in a losing position.

While you want your investment managers to have confidence in their research and methods, you also want them to exhibit a good degree of humility and to be able to admit when they are wrong. I've seen far too many portfolios die at the altar of a stubborn belief in rising inflation, interest rates, gold prices, or, worst of all, a strategy dependent on anticipating another market crash—another 1929, 1974, or 2000. If your portfolio's success depends on events that take place only a few times each century, you are on the wrong path, playing a low-probability game.

A manager who has committed publicly to a strong opinion on a certain asset (for example, "oil is going to $200 a barrel" or "the US dollar will inevitably collapse") is a huge red flag. Once you have publicly, and often very visibly, committed yourself to a certain viewpoint, it becomes far more difficult to disavow this position in the future without losing face. You'll find that money managers in this position will often stick to their public views far longer than they should, ignoring any contrary evidence, if only as part of refusing to admit they were wrong. Don't let their ego take you along for the ride.

Conviction is not a one-time thing. Your conviction needs to be tested by constant enquiry and skepticism. Premeditatio malorum. Question. Debate. Discuss and think things through. If it's instead driven by a religious fervor, causing you to dismiss contrary information out of hand, then it can be a dangerous thing. Now we're heading into "blind faith" territory.

So I'm calling on you to make sure you have conviction in your manager, who in turn has conviction in their strategy. But I'm also asking you to beware of the impact of ego, and of having blind faith in a manager or strategy that may not have earned that confidence. Indeed, the more confident a manager appears in public, often, the more that confidence is masking tremendous insecurity and uncertainty. It's a delicate balance. But being aware of it is an important part of the process.

Developing conviction in your manager

At this point you might be thinking, *This is great, but how am I to gain conviction in a manager or strategy if I know very little about investing?*

You can't escape the need to have conviction, because without it you risk being shaken out of your investments at the worst possible time.

So, short of becoming a financial analyst in your spare time, what can you do?

First of all, immediately address any nagging doubts you have in your portfolio, the manager, or the strategy being employed. Because these minor doubts will be screaming at you in a downturn. Address them when markets are calm. Speak with your advisor or portfolio manager. Make sure you understand what they are trying to do, and the role that each investment plays in this objective. And if you're not satisfied with what you're hearing, the time to change strategies is *now*. Don't wait for markets to find themselves in turmoil before you decide to act. You will almost certainly end up selling at the wrong time.

It's also important to make sure that your expectations are reasonable. Chasing top-tier performance or insisting on outperformance in all market environments is the root of all investment failure. You will inevitably end up jumping on trends as they peak, and bailing on investments just before they come back into favor. I'm not saying you should tolerate sustained underperformance, but make sure to evaluate your managers over a long enough period of time, and don't be afraid to stick with them if underperformance is driven by extenuating circumstances.

I've worked with clients in the past who have an idea in their heads that they can somehow optimize their portfolio. They've obviously sat through too many academic finance presentations. Outside of finance textbooks, there is no such thing as an optimized portfolio.

To be clear, there are many permutations of shitty portfolios, but much rarer are those that are built for what you are actually trying to accomplish.

Chasing perfection will be a constant source of unhappiness. If I left my wife each time I met someone who might be able to tolerate my taste in music or my crappy dishwasher-loading skills, I'd be eternally unhappy. Not to mention that I'd miss all of the things that attracted me to her in the first place.

You need to decide what's important to *you*, and focus on that.

I gain conviction by acknowledging that I *can't* optimize the portfolio; so, rather, I try to reduce the number of variables at play. If I can just own great companies that I purchased at decent prices and hold for the long term, that is how I gain my conviction.

Better—hire an advisor or portfolio manager who understands you, builds a portfolio that serves you, and helps you develop the conviction you need in your strategy.

When it comes to investment success, your ability to stick with a strategy can matter more than the strategy itself.

Conviction is the key.

22

TAKE RESPONSIBILITY

Whatever.

ME, *when my wife asks what I want for dinner*

The flimsy foundation of academic finance

The small investor of today can credit Jack Bogle, founder of the Vanguard Group, for popularizing the index fund.

The index fund emerged from humble beginnings in the mid-1970s, and at the time few realized how huge a victory it was for small investors. Think about it—before Vanguard, there were gatekeepers standing between you and the stock market, extracting prodigious amounts of juice from your portfolio. If you're young enough, you probably don't know that the full-service stockbroker used to be the only way for individuals to buy stocks directly, and they actually charged hundreds of dollars for each trade. Then came the mutual fund, which allowed for diversification of small accounts but at a cost of 2 or 3 percent per year on your money.

Bogle is a hero because he dropped an atomic bomb on this racket. Like Jesus kicking the money-changers out of the temple, he played a large part in cleaning up an industry that put itself before its clients. He gave small investors an opportunity to diversify their holdings in a low-cost fund and preached a gospel of common sense with easy-to-follow rules.

Creating an ultra-low-cost, purely passive investment vehicle for the everyman was a shot across the bow of the financial industry. For the small investor, I would argue that it remains the preferred solution to build portfolios, despite its flaws.

In order to have an informed opinion on passive investing as a strategy, it's important to understand the basic premise behind it, and that's going to require us to go down the rabbit hole of academic finance.

(Just as an aside, you may have a hard time finding a money manager who admits to implementing a passive strategy for you these days. The idea of paying someone to invest "passively" on your behalf didn't really sell well, and so these strategies have been re-branded as "evidence based investing." By the time you read this, they may have some other nomenclature attached to them. For the sake of consistency, I refer to them all as academic finance–based strategies.)

Passive investing is based on a theory called the Efficient Market Hypothesis (EMH), upon which most academic finance rests. The hypothesis states that, at any given time, share prices reflect all publicly available information. If EMH is true, then we shouldn't try to pick individual stocks.

As the EMH theory goes, there are millions of investors around the world, all trying to find mispriced stocks. Through all of their buying and selling, the cumulative impact of their research is reflected in market prices.

For example, if enough people think that Microsoft is expensive, they will sell the stock. If others think it's cheap, they will buy the stock. The equilibrium point, where the stock currently trades, is theoretically the "correct" value for the company, reflecting all publicly available information. So you can save yourself the effort of trying to pick stocks. Just buy everything and go along for the ride.

Through the EMH we were introduced to the concept of index investing, which has been a tremendous force for good, democratizing investing for the masses and bringing down unnecessary expenses. For the small investor, it's hard to recommend any investment strategy other than a low-cost index fund or ETF. Even large institutional investors often index vast portions of their equity portfolios in an effort to capture the stock market return with the lowest possible costs. (This is what they call earning "beta," and remember what I said about running away when they start with the Greek letters?)

This book isn't for small investors. And it isn't for institutional investors. And so I'm going to explain where passive investing goes wrong for most wealthy private clients.

A full critique of the EMH is beyond the scope of this book, but suffice it to say that even "passive" investors who hang their proverbial hat on this theory make adjustments to its practical application. Many things get in the way of a "pure" EMH existing in the real world, including behavioral investing quirks, transaction costs, and the impact of insider information, to name a few.

In fact, the same group of researchers that developed the EMH went on to identify a couple of major anomalies that have persisted over time. Anomalies that, if their claims of market efficiency were correct, *should not exist.*

The first is the "small firm" anomaly, which states that, over long periods of time, the shares of smaller companies outperform those of larger companies.

The second major anomaly is the "low book value" or "value" anomaly, which shows outperformance for the shares of companies that trade at a low multiple of "book" value (the carrying value of assets on the company's balance sheet).

Even though these anomalies were identified a long time ago, they have persisted for decades, which doesn't make sense if you believe in the EMH, right? After all, the public knowledge that they exist should be enough to cause investors to bid up the prices of small value companies, eliminating the ability to earn excess returns by investing in them! So the academic finance guys have spent decades trying to explain why these anomalies exist.

In the meantime, though, they play along. Given the persistence of these anomalies, they have actually been incorporated in what is commonly known as the Three Factor Model, where academic finance practitioners will recommend a very diversified portfolio with a "tilt" towards what they call the small company and value factors, in order to capture the premium offered by these factors.

In fact, I think by 2014 they introduced a Five Factor Model. Apparently there are more factors being discovered. Like asteroids. As you're reading this, academics are formulating a Six Factor Model.

In *The (Mis)Behavior of Markets*, mathematician Benoit Mandelbrot ruthlessly demolishes academic finance by demonstrating that the models on which it is built are dangerously simplified. He writes:

> And the high priests of modern financial theory keep moving the target. As each anomaly is reported, a "fix" is made to accommodate it ... But such ad hoc fixes are medieval. They work around, rather than build from and explain, the contradictory evidence ... So again, why does the old order continue? Habit and convenience. The math is, at bottom, easy and can be made to look impressive, inscrutable to all but the rocket scientist. Business schools around the world keep teaching it. They have trained thousands of financial

officers, thousands of investment advisers. In fact, as most of these graduates learn from subsequent experience, it does not work as advertised; and they develop myriad ad hoc improvements, adjustments, and accommodations to get the jobs done. But still, it gives a comforting impression of precision and competence.

In my experience, all of the tinkering and analysis of academic finance appeals to a specific type of person. I especially find that scientists and engineers appreciate the supporting data behind the theory, and that, as in science itself, the research rests on constant advancement and falsifiability. For the right person, the anomalies are a *feature*, not a bug. If this is you, and this is an investment strategy you can believe in, that's awesome.

I find that for most people, and especially for investment novices and entrepreneurs, academic finance does not resonate. Academic finance takes something simple (owning a piece of a business) and complicates it with mathematical formulas, incoherent graphs, and Greek letters.

Some anomalies are durable. Most are ephemeral. As soon as they are discovered and made public, they no longer work. Constantly adapting your portfolio to chase these temporary anomalies is another risk of putting too much faith in academic finance.

I think most people are looking for something more durable. Not research that changes conclusions several times over a lifetime, but rather—and almost like religion—a timeless set of principles. Luckily, it actually exists. And it's also been supported by research. Sounds like the best of both worlds.

Not choosing is a choice

In recent years, technology has enabled an ever-greater pro-liferation of specialty funds, many of them based on various academic studies. As these strategies have hit the mainstream via various funds and ETFs, a divide has widened within the wealth management industry—those who believe in active management on one side, implemented through the purchase of individual company shares, and passive advocates on the other, implemented through various mutual funds and ETFs.

I'm trying not to turn this into an active versus passive debate, because I believe that the argument is largely noise. If you really stop to think about it, you realize that there's actu-ally no such thing as passive investing. Because just like you eventually need to make a choice of what to have for dinner, you can't avoid making a choice in what you're invested in.

Sure, I can just call the restaurant and tell them to send over "whatever," but I still need to decide which restaurant to call.

This is not a trivial matter. Deciding how your portfolio is invested is important, because it determines how your port-folio is going to behave next time the market goes down. And you'll need to be ready to deal with it.

If I say I don't care what I eat, it's because in my mind I'm anticipating a decision between pizza and burgers. Honestly, I'm good with either. But if I say "whatever," and I'm pre-sented with a dish of grilled tofu and kale, I can't complain. I need to eat the tofu and kale. It's going to be hard. I'm going to regret every bite. But it's what I signed up for.

Similarly, at a very basic level you're going to need to decide on a strategy for your investment portfolio, and if you say "whatever" and go with whatever product is being pushed at the time you open your account, you may have to choke down some very difficult returns when the market turns against you (because it always does). Or you'll end up bailing on the strategy and selling after a big decline, just like all of those investors in the CGM Focus Fund.

Pay no attention to the man behind the curtain

Apart from all of the factors that cause us to question the veracity of the Efficient Market Hypothesis, the process of indexing itself has several problems. Yes, it's a great solution for small investors whose only other choice is often costly funds sold through their bank branch, but it leaves much to be desired for larger investors.

There's a romantic notion around passive investing that you're buying the entire market with one purchase. With the single click of a mouse, you now own a diversified basket of the world's largest and most successful companies.

The reality is a bit more nuanced. Have you ever considered who decides which stocks end up in the index? Well, in the case of the S&P 500, it's a committee that meets once a quarter. Want to know who's on the committee? You can't. Apart from the chair, it's a secret. And yes, I'm totally serious about that.

There are some rules around which companies get in and which don't, but there is a lot of subjectivity involved as well, and so the committee votes on who's in and who's out—majority rules. In the case of a tie, they continue to hash it out until one anonymous member sways to the other side.

Getting included in the S&P 500 is kind of a big deal. According to S&P Global, there is about $13.5 trillion benchmarked to the index at the time of this writing. So the act of substituting one company with another one has the potential impact of transferring billions of dollars of share ownership in a short period of time. The power afforded to an anonymous indexing committee is, quite frankly, astonishing.

You might suppose this isn't such a big deal as long as there is very little turnover in the index. It would be fair to assume that decisions of this sort would be very rare.

You would be wrong about that. Since the S&P 500 as we currently know it was created in 1957, only sixty of the original 500 constituents remain. Notably, turnover in the index is increasing, with the average tenure declining from thirty-three years in 1964 to an estimated twelve years in 2027.

So it's critically important for the passive investor to know that the decision they have made is for their portfolio to be determined by a largely anonymous committee that votes on a majority rules basis. Other than the fact that the S&P 500 (and the vast majority of other indices) own an unwieldy number of stocks, this isn't quite as "passive" as you might have imagined.

I've focused on the S&P 500, but other indices work in much the same manner. And whether there's a committee behind it or a set of automated rules, inclusion in the index originates with a person, or group of people, who decide which stocks are in, and which stocks are out—through either judgment or a set of preprogrammed automated rules.

That's the first thing you need to know about investing in an index. When you get down to it, it's based on many of the same principles as the active management that its proponents spend so much time denigrating. At some point, someone, somewhere, is making a choice to include one company, while excluding another. And in the case of the S&P 500, you don't even know who these people are!

Another complicating factor is the huge proliferation of indices that have arisen from the ETF mania. So much so that, in May of 2017, *Bloomberg* magazine famously announced that "there are now more indices than stocks." Those who choose to pursue a "passive" strategy are therefore faced with the very difficult decision of which indices to buy. As you can see, the so-called "democratization" of investing has quickly devolved into a very complex area where most people will need some sort of professional guidance.

Now here's the one argument I agree with: that, via indexing, you have the ability to keep your costs as low as possible. You're buying an arbitrary basket of stocks, and therefore don't have to worry about the costs of detailed research. As the theory goes, this makes up for the variability in results you might see with an active manager. And because the total market return is the average of the returns experienced by all market participants—and they're paying for research, which passive investors aren't—this is incontrovertibly true.

However, for reasons I'm about to explain, I believe that pursuing a purely passive approach is a poor choice for most people reading this book.

Shitty indices

A big problem with indexing is—and please excuse my use of the technical finance term—shitty indices.

I'm Canadian, and this is a big issue up here. As I write this, if you decide to create a passive portfolio tracking the Toronto Exchange benchmark, you've made the decision to hold an abnormally high allocation to bank stocks, energy companies, and gold miners. Your health care allocation is basically just cannabis stocks. And your technology sector exposure is focused around two companies. Your largest position for most of the past year was Shopify, which is a great company but an expensive, momentum-driven stock whose volatility makes it difficult to own for many people. (At the time of writing, it has fallen almost 50 percent in just two months, which kinda proves my point.)

And lest you think I'm cherry-picking a particular data set, at various times in the past your "passive" allocation to Canadian equities saw your largest position being in stocks like Valeant Pharmaceuticals (which was subsequently censured for fraud and accounting tricks) and Nortel (a wildly overvalued telecommunications stock in the tech bubble that never actually generated any free cash flow). Both of these stocks subsequently declined by over 90 percent. Nortel was a zero.

Basically, what I'm trying to get at is that the Canadian equity benchmark is a shitty index, and you don't want to have much of your wealth in it. If you are invested in it, you need to know that you're highly levered to oil and commodity prices. In your effort not to choose investments (by implementing a passive strategy), this is the economic exposure that you have chosen.

I'm picking on Canada only because I know it so well, but any number of countries that rely heavily on a single industry or multinational company will have the same issue. Passively investing in their benchmarks is a bad idea, because the benchmarks themselves are shitty.

It is at these times, and in these markets, when buying indices is a horrible idea. When you aren't buying a well-diversified basket of stocks at all, but one or a few highly correlated large companies or one large industry that dominates index movements. That's a shitty index, full stop.

The other problem you may have picked out is that the largest companies and sectors in any given index will change over time. It usually happens around market tops, when "hot" industry groups and companies make up a dangerously large percentage of the index. As I'm writing this, the S&P 500 is dominated by Apple, Microsoft, Amazon, Meta, and Google, which together represent around 25 percent of the index. Now, these are all huge, powerful companies that generate strong cash flows. But they are also the drivers of market performance, and consequently have become central to a huge momentum trade. So someone buying the s&p 500 is making a bet on these companies' shares continuing to defy gravity—and there's no way around that. In trying to be "passive," you have made the decision to believe that the prices of these five stocks will continue to rise unabated.

The s&p 500, which is the main benchmark used by us stock investors, from time to time can become a shitty index.

This isn't unprecedented, and it seems to happen mostly around market tops, when investors are at their most ebullient. In 1973, the market was dominated by the "Nifty Fifty," which, similar to today's technology superstars, were being purchased by investors at any price. Avon at 61x earnings? Check. Polaroid at 94x? Yep. Disney at 71x? Load up the truck.

The subsequent 1973/74 market decline remains one of the worst drawdowns on record.

So when you buy an index, what exactly are you buying?

If you're a Canadian who bought the TSX Composite any time in the past ten years, you're rolling the dice between having a 10 percent or a 25 percent energy allocation. And counter to what you should be doing (buying low and selling high), you'll buy more when the sector is expensive, and less when it's cheap.

Buying high and selling low.

If you bought the s&p 500 in 2014, you had a 14 percent allocation to technology. If you bought the same index in 2020, just six years later, you had a 28 percent allocation to the same sector, and at much higher valuations. That's a wild swing. Do you know what it means for your portfolio volatility and risk? Do you know if it's appropriate for you?

And if the s&p 500, the mother of all indices, can become shitty, what hope is there for the rest of them? And if formerly good indices can become shitty slowly and imperceptibly over time, are you really comfortable relying on a passive approach to protect your wealth?

Too often, and usually at precisely the wrong time, indexing steers investors into more concentrated, momentum-driven trades, increasing risk.

Who is watching your "passive" investments for you?

A problem with passive investing is that, to do it well, you actually need to be more active than anyone lets on. It's ultimately active management, implemented through baskets of stocks chosen for you by anonymous committees and automated criteria.

Is your advisor making sure to adjust your risk exposure as the makeup of these indices changes, and as their risk increases?

If so, you're probably paying for it, which may negate the supposed cost advantages of the passive approach.

There is no such thing as truly passive investing. And that's a good thing.

No responsibility, no conviction

Just to be clear, I'm not solidly against academic finance-based strategies—if their wide diversification and theoretical underpinnings give you comfort and conviction, they will perform quite well over time. And I definitely prefer them to most overly diversified and expensive allocator portfolios. But for me, it all rings a bit hollow and would make me question my strategy at the worst times. Sure, it's wonderful when the market is rising, but it's harder to believe in when everything is falling. When I need that conviction the most, I would find myself grasping for it.

Passive investing is great because you own every high-flying, market-beating stock.

But passive investing can also suck because you own a bunch of crappy companies, including frauds and bubble stocks. And if your passive basket is market-weighted, you own more of the companies that are relatively expensive.

One of the strengths of passive investing is also one of the weaknesses of passive investing, and all you have to do is change the punctuation.

Pro: "You own a piece of every company."

Con: "You own a piece of every company?"

Maybe in the future we will look back and wonder how we thought it was a good idea to buy everything, without any thought to price, value, or quality.

I'm not saying we *will*. I'm just saying we *might*.

And that's enough to shake my conviction.

If you want conviction, you need to take responsibility.

23

KNOW WHAT YOU OWN

If you are going to be a great investor,
you have to fit the style to who you are.

MICHAEL J. BURRY

The problem with academic finance

The academics will spend all sorts of time looking for an edge.

A few will find something effective and make some money off it. But once it becomes well known, the assets get bid up and the edge basically disappears. They don't ring a bell to let you know when that happens . . . it just does. By the time an idea gets to you, it's likely over.

So now academic finance just becomes about capturing the market return in the most efficient way (read: lowest cost).

This is awesome, and I'm totally in favor of it.

But then something happens.

A speculative bubble pops.

There's a mortgage crisis.

Maybe a global pandemic.

A loss of confidence in the system.

And you don't truly understand what's in your portfolio.

You sell at the wrong time.

You lose.

The fundamental problem with academic finance is that it's for research journals and textbooks. It's not for you.

And here's why.

Active management shapes entrepreneurial conviction

The academic finance guys are right about a lot. Because their strategies are often based on decades of research, it would be foolish to dismiss them out of hand.

So while I agree that many of their criticisms of active management are correct, I also think they miss the point.

I'm about to tell you a secret about investing, and it might surprise you based on the marketing material and propaganda you've been subject to from all sides in this debate over the years.

There is no right way to invest.

There is no strategy that guarantees success.

What works for someone else might not work for you at all.

Remember when I said conviction is the key? Well, the best strategy for you is the one you will have the most conviction in.

Note that I didn't say the best strategy is the one that will outperform. Or the one that will have the highest risk-adjusted return. Or the one that costs the least. All of these are noble objectives to pursue in building a portfolio, but without *your* conviction, they are not right for you.

There's a saying among professional investors—"you can't borrow conviction." The idea is that I can steal stock picks from anyone, but I can't steal their conviction in the investment. So if you follow a respected manager into a particular stock, you have to be aware that you won't know when they decide to sell, or if their opinion has changed. If things turn south (which they inevitably will at some point), you must have your own conviction in order to decide to hold on, or to buy more. If the facts change (which they will), you alone need to know how this shapes your confidence in the investment and whether it's time to change your thesis.

The same applies to the wealth manager you hire—how well do you understand their strategy? How confident are you in it? Let's exercise some premeditatio malorum and decide if this is a strategy we are willing to ride out when the going gets tough.

Most people I've worked with over the years—entrepreneurs and professionals—simply don't understand academic finance-based strategies. How do I know that? Because I've been doing this for over two decades, and I've talked to people who shrug at the various passive and academic based funds in their portfolios.

And I don't blame them! I often zone out when researchers start droning on about factors and explaining derivations of formulas. I have a hard time believing that people with no formal finance training care to take the time necessary to truly understand how their portfolio is being built.

So it all comes down to your advisor saying "trust me." And trusting your advisor isn't a bad thing (as long as you're trusting a knowledgeable and trustworthy person). The problem comes when your investment performance starts to sag, and you start to wonder if you're in the right strategies with the right advisor, and you suddenly realize you don't really understand what's in those funds in your portfolio. And so what happens is that your faith is shaken at the exact worst time. When your portfolio is down and forward-looking potential returns are at their highest, you sell. As illustrated in the Dalbar study, it's a recipe for long-term underperformance. And it's a tragically common tale. Every advisor will tell you that their phone starts ringing during and after a market decline, when investors lose confidence in their current advisors and portfolios.

If you don't understand something, you can't have conviction in it. It will be that much harder to hold on when you need to.

The index that I bought several years, or decades, ago, is not the same any more. The constituents have changed. The largest companies in the index have changed. What I bought that may have once been dominated by conservative health care and financial companies might today be mostly driven by the performance of high-flying technology shares trading at stratospheric valuations. The index itself may have become more volatile and risky over time.

When I need to buy more, am I ready to do so? Or is there something in the back of my mind making me question what I'm invested in? Is it possible that I own a shitty index? Can I trust this anonymous committee's decisions?

On the other hand, if I own an actively managed portfolio, I can see the names of the companies I'm invested in. I can talk to the portfolio manager about what we own and why we own it. I can gain some reassurance that my largest holdings can survive a prolonged recession, that their balance sheets are strong, and, in fact, that they stand to gain market share against weaker competitors, regardless of market conditions.

Now I have *conviction*. And now I can gain the confidence to hold on at the bottom. I can gain the confidence to allocate more to equities when things look their most bleak.

This is why I believe in active management. Not because of an expectation to outperform a passive benchmark—there is no guarantee of that. I believe in active management because it is the best way I know for an investor—particularly an entrepreneurial investor—to gain the conviction they need to stick with their plan when it's hardest to do so.

I'm not saying that having an active manager is the *only* way an investor can have conviction in their portfolio. But I am saying that, in my experience, for the vast majority of people it's the *best* way for an investor to have conviction in their portfolio.

Why do I say this?

I work with many people who have created their wealth by building (and often selling) a business. The academic finance crew might say that it's "optimal" to put your money in a passive, factor-weighted portfolio, but that would ignore the fact that you are an entrepreneur.

You probably appreciate knowing that your investment strategy is built on the foundation of owning businesses—it's how you made your wealth. But just owning baskets of hundreds or thousands of businesses doesn't necessarily resonate. You admire quality management teams. You appreciate their stories. You may also like to have some level of control over your portfolio—for example, excluding certain companies or sectors, or overweighting others. And so I find that it's harder for entrepreneurs to gain conviction in passive strategies.

If the stock market is down 40 percent, I might be really nervous about the performance of my XYZCO AlphaOmega Small-Mid-Large Cap Value-Growth ETF, even if it's down only 30 percent. But if my shares of Johnson & Johnson are down 30 percent, I'm more likely to stick with the plan, and, in fact, even buy more shares. Because I know that J&J ain't going anywhere.

Without conviction, the market will shake you out of your investments at the worst possible time.

Outperformance is not the point

While I believe that active management is an important element to creating conviction for the entrepreneur, many are surprised to hear that I don't also believe that active management can reliably outperform passive strategies.

The HNW Industrial Complex loves using allocators to build portfolios for wealthy investors. And allocators build portfolios based on the idea of selecting active managers with various specialties. These consultants will introduce you to "the best" small-cap, large-cap, global, US, or emerging market equity managers. And in all my years of working with these consultants, through direct experience as a client and also through working with estates, foundations, and pension committees, I have found that they are full of shit. I haven't seen any reliable indication that any consultant can identify outperforming managers. And, as discussed in Chapter 10, research backs that claim up.

And lest you think I'm being unfair, I'll include myself in the mix. I did have some success selecting managers in the past. But it didn't come from reviewing charts and tables, which is the method preferred by the consulting industry. Rather, it came from meeting with the managers and their teams, hearing their stories and gauging the passion they had for investing. I did find some exceptional managers, but my sample size isn't large enough to attribute it to anything other than luck. I say this not to be modest, but because I know that I also found managers who said all the right things, conferred the appropriate level of confidence, and yet still failed to keep up with their passive benchmarks over large stretches of time. One hedge fund manager I was particularly enthusiastic about (and who, thankfully, my clients did not end up allocating capital to) ended up closing his fund within two years of our initial meeting.

So when the academic finance brigade tells us that we can't reliably select the managers who will outperform in the future, I agree with them wholeheartedly.

But that's not the point.

The point is conviction.

Hopefully, outperformance will be a byproduct of that conviction, by giving you a strategy you can stick with through thick and thin.

And active management shapes entrepreneurial conviction.

24

IT'S ART, NOT SCIENCE

Investing in stocks is an art, not a science,
and people who've been trained to rigidly quantify
everything have a big disadvantage.

PETER LYNCH

How to implement it

There's something glaringly, obviously wrong with my endorsement of the low-risk anomaly, and I'm sure that "evidence based" academic finance practitioners are shaking their fists at me and calling me a hypocrite.

You see, the low-risk anomaly is itself an academic finance construct—derived from decades of study and observation. And it's been tested by creating rigid, academic finance–based rules. Now an automated, rules-based approach is a fine way to implement a low-risk investing strategy. But I don't think it's the *best* way to implement a low-risk investing strategy.

Why do I say this?

Recall that market anomalies are ephemeral. The more easily they can be replicated, the more likely they are to stop working. As with any anomaly, once we try to turn a low-risk

237

strategy into a set of rigid trading rules, it can be easily repli-cated and could thereby lose its effectiveness over time.

So the first problem is that I need to define "low risk," which the research does by defining it in terms of volatility. This is necessary because empirical study requires an objec-tive and consistent risk measurement that can be used across different markets.

There is an obvious problem with this, and if you've been following along you already know what it is.

It's fundamental to the theme of this book.

And it comes down to the definition of risk. More specifi-cally, *your* definition of risk.

Here it is: volatility is not risk!

To be clear, volatility is risk to the extent that it can throw you off your investment plan by forcing you into mistakes. But stock price volatility, in and of itself, lies. Remember—the volatility you see is lying to you. Volatility in itself is not a risk to a long-term fundamental investor (that's you!). *Your* risk measure is preserving your purchasing power over time, not any academic definition of risk.

OK—so if low risk isn't necessarily low volatility, how should we define it?

I've said it before, and I'll say it again: you are building your portfolio out of businesses, not stocks. Let the academic finance guys define low-risk stocks as those that exhibit low price volatility. That's fine. While they are building portfolios out of stocks, we will build empires out of businesses.

So, how to define low-risk businesses?

As I have implored you to do, let's carry your business skills into the investment realm. What is a low-risk investment? Think like a businessperson. Forget price volatility. A low-risk business would have consistent cash flows. Pricing power. Low debt. It's selling an essential product or service to a diversified customer base. It has some sort of sustainable advantage over its competitors, in a business with high barriers to entry. If you were designing a business from scratch with a primary goal of protecting your wealth, think of the characteristics you'd like your business to have. Invest in companies that share those defensive characteristics.

Now you've got a portfolio of low-risk businesses. And here's where we tie it all together with a bow. It just so happens that companies exhibiting these defensive, low-risk characteristics also tend to have lower price volatility and lower beta, also fitting into the academic "low risk" bucket. Not always, but usually. And so your "low-risk business" empire will end up looking a lot like a "low-risk stock" portfolio.

This is why I can feel comfortable leaning on the academic research, and extrapolating it through to a fundamental bottom-up portfolio of businesses.

So, what are the key differences between the two approaches?

First, you'll own fewer businesses, because there are only so many that your portfolio manager can keep on top of and understand. An academic strategy, on the other hand, sees stocks as commodities and will hold hundreds or thousands of different names. The benefit to you is that you'll have a better understanding of what your money manager owns in your account, which will help you maintain conviction in the strategy.

Second, you may end up owning a few businesses that the market perceives as higher risk, but that your portfolio manager understands to be lower risk. This is the essence of value investing—identifying a situation where Mr. Market misunderstands the true value of an underlying business. This allows a skilled money manager to add value to your portfolio over time... by stocking up on "lower risk" situations which the market incorrectly perceives are "higher risk."

As you can tell, this value approach entails the use of judg-ment. Variable skill (and luck!) levels between managers mean that you can't automate the process and can't rely on the consistency of the results. Some investors may find this unacceptable, but my contention is that investing relies on human behavior and will therefore always be an art, not a sci-ence. Investors must be comfortable with uncertainty. But as an entrepreneur you should have no problem with that. It's in your water.

Besides, strictly rules-based approaches come with their own problems. Sometimes they cause you to take risks you didn't necessarily intend to take. For example, passive value strategies often emphasize measures like book value, which could lead to a heavy allocation to banks and insurance companies, which may not always be appropriate (it's why many value funds did poorly in the 2008/09 mortgage cri-sis). Low-priced value stocks may also carry low prices for a reason—that is, their business is struggling, or in a dying industry, or the company has been mismanaged. Cyclical companies also appear to be cheap at the top of a business cycle, and buying them based simply on a low P/E ratio, as an automated value strategy might, can be dangerous.

Similarly, low-volatility funds rely on a series of rules to qualify stocks for the portfolio that are based on historical observed volatility, which may not match the volatility we see in the future. Worse, as this strategy becomes more or less popular over time, the performance can actually be impacted by fund flows in and out of stocks that exhibit these trading characteristics.

In plain English, this means that decisions other investors are making can turn low-volatility stocks into high-volatility stocks over time, which might offset any of the benefits you're trying to achieve.

Unfortunately, the quest for a passive, low-cost, rules-based approach to investing often leads to these kinds of dead ends. Because markets are dynamic, you can't really switch your portfolio onto autopilot and ignore what's going on around you. You need someone watching the road ahead. For all of these reasons, I believe that it's far better to build a portfolio made up of low-risk businesses than just focus on low-risk stocks. The end result may be very similar, but you can have far more confidence in the implementation, and thereby have more conviction in your portfolio.

I believe that by creating a portfolio of low-risk businesses, which as a group exhibit the characteristics of a low-volatility portfolio (but individually may not), you are getting the best of all worlds.

That's a winning low-risk approach.

Why we focus on quality

To be clear, what I'm talking about here is a fairly typical value investing strategy, but bound by a low-risk framework. This is going to make it easier to execute and easier to gain conviction in, and therefore easier to stick with over time.

True unbound value investing can get messy, because value investors are a unique breed. Most hardcore value investors love searching for bargains in deep, dark, forgotten corners of the market. As an investing geek, I share their enthusiasm for uncovering an unknown gem that promises a huge potential payoff with very little downside risk.

But this is a game for advanced investors, and for clients who are comfortable with the risk involved. It's generally not a place the novice investor should have their money staked.

One of the main risks to this type of strategy is illiquidity. These days, searching for value can take you into micro-cap land, investing in tiny unknown companies. Or it can take you overseas into obscure, hard-to-access stock markets. It is often easier to build positions in these companies than it is to sell them. And that can be a problem if your investment thesis doesn't pan out. That introduces illiquidity as a risk factor, and can make it seem almost like investing in private equity.

Second, being led by a portfolio manager into difficult or esoteric strategies, or into obscure global market corners, can make it more challenging to have conviction in what you own. My portfolio manager can tell me that this company I own is one of the leading detergent brands in Indonesia, but if I've never done my laundry in Jakarta, I may have a hard time believing in the durability of the company when my portfolio is getting beat up.

Then there are the deep-value investors looking for troubled companies trading cheap. These are often called "cigar butts," the theory being that there are always a few puffs left in a discarded cigar. This can be a profitable game, but it's a dangerous one. And it's hard to gain conviction in a portfolio full of admittedly struggling businesses, no matter how cheap they may be. Also, the idea of puffing on someone else's discarded cigar is gross. You didn't work your whole life for that.

A quality-focused low-risk approach is a way to build a value portfolio in a more straightforward way and in safer areas of the market. Easier for novice investors to understand. Easier for them to stick with. Once again, we are back to the concept of conviction, and how important it is in crafting your portfolio.

And so, for most people new to the game, or without intense interest in the details of investing, I recommend keeping it simple and high quality.

This approach takes the best of value and low-volatility investing and combines them into an approach that entrepreneurs can appreciate as a way to preserve and grow wealth.

We're buying pieces of mature, stable, dominant businesses at attractive prices and holding on for the long term. We're hiring their managers to partner with us in taking care of your wealth.

The rules are clear, and they work. But sometimes you just gotta adapt them to make your own rules.

This is how you're going to construct a moat around your wealth.

This is how you're going to build your empire.

CONCLUSION
LET GO AND ACT BOLDLY

---

*The secret is to win going
as slowly as possible.*
NIKI LAUDA

Why make it so hard?

The opening quote for this chapter has been attributed to various F1 drivers, but seems to have first been said by Niki Lauda, three-time World Drivers' Champion for both Ferrari and McLaren. Whipping around a track at awesome speeds, professional drivers are uniquely qualified to comment on risk. And just as I began by reminding you to play your own game, I'm going to wrap up by reminding you that you are in your own race. You have your own objectives, and you are driving on your own track.

Taking driving advice from others doesn't make any sense. Going faster than necessary, or taking more risk than necessary, just increases the odds that you don't finish the race. And if you don't finish, you can't win.

Entrepreneurial life can at times feel completely out of control. Just like a car careening around the track, the driver barely in control at the limits. Driver skill intervenes to regain control more than once. And yes, luck also plays an occasional role in preventing a catastrophic crash.

The game is different now. It's a new race, and it should be an easier one. You just need to adapt your driving style to the new track.

Always remember how things could have turned out differently, and how fortunate you are to be right here, right now.

Switch to defense. Diversify. Create your safety net.

Keep your eyes on the horizon, locked on your North Star. Don't let the salespeople and their false promises convince you to drive a more difficult track. Don't be misled by short-term volatility, scared by the media's fear mongering, or tempted to chase the fashionable investments of the day.

Remember that you are an investor, and that there is no magic to allocating capital—only the same common-sense principles that got you here. You know more about investing than the salespeople, or the financial reporters.

Guard yourself against high fees, needless complexity, and anything designed to trap your capital in investments that pay off only in bragging rights.

Play your own game, at your own pace. Don't worry about how rich everyone else is getting, or how panicked they all appear to be over the headlines of the day.

Invest, don't speculate. Understand your investment edge and honor it.

Gain conviction in a strategy that resonates with you, working with an advisor who understands what you're trying to achieve and is dedicated to helping you get there.

It doesn't have to be as difficult as many make it out to be, and if someone is making it seem that way, they are probably trying to sell you something.

So... armed with the knowledge that you can do better over time with a low-risk portfolio, are you destined for a life of trouble-free investment success?

If you're wise enough to leave well enough alone, and lucky enough to hire the right money manager, you might do very well.

Counterintuitively, the more engaged you are in the process, the closer you follow financial markets, and the more actively you try to add value, the worse you'll do.

How do I know this? Because despite being armed with the knowledge described in this book, and applying it faithfully for my own clients, I am often unable to behave properly when it comes to my own money. I cheat. I buy riskier stocks. I've tried shorting ridiculously overvalued stocks and markets. I do this despite knowing everything that I've described in this book.

I've had some big winners. I've had some painful losses. The net impact has been a lot more stress in my life, a distraction from the things I should be focusing on, and probably a reduction in my own net worth.

In all honesty, while I'm writing this book for you, it's equally a reminder to myself to stick to the proven process I've outlined.

Why do we do this? When we know how to win the game, why do we make it so much harder?

We're looking for a challenge.

We love the thrill.

We dream about the profits on our next trade, and what it could buy us.

But it's like playing off the pro tees as a beginning golfer. What exactly are we trying to prove?

Trading successfully is a game that requires you to always be a step ahead of other investors. In the buying, and the selling. From one stock to the next. Dropping today's hot theme for the next one. It's a constant treadmill, and it runs faster and faster as you go.

The whole process can be exhausting.

Not to mention nearly impossible to execute successfully.

It's not something you can do in your spare time, or as a hobby. Because your competition is working on it 24/7.

We know there's an easier way to invest. Why do we insist on making it so hard?

Let go

After reviewing all of this evidence, you might be asking yourself why low-risk remains such an unpopular investment strategy.

The cold, hard truth is that it just doesn't sell.

There are a million and one quick diet fixes pitched online, but no mass market for the message that eating whole, natural foods and keeping active is the way to long-term health.

The truth can be boring and doesn't quite inspire action like the false promises do. The road is long, and navigating it takes time and patience. There is no such thing as overnight success.

Investing is no different. You're being sold a quick-fix diet. Or an expensive health club membership that might get you in the right social circles but won't do much to help the spare tire around your waist. The salespeople are not telling you the truth because it's not in their interest to do so. And let's be honest, you don't want to hear it, either.

The road to success in investing is actually far easier than you think it is. Unlike embarking on a rigorous training regimen and a strict diet, all you need to do is ignore the crowd. Be happy with a very boring portfolio invested in dominant companies that compounds slowly, over time. Know you're on the right path. And do nothing. Honestly, that's all there is to it.

There's a universal truth reflected in this strategy. Success often requires you to let go.

Grip your golf club too hard and the tension will be reflected in your entire swing. Your shot is likely to end up off target.

Put too much pressure on yourself to pass a test and you're sure to make dumb mistakes.

Try too hard to impress on the first date and there likely won't be a second.

It's the paradox of trying too hard.

The same thing applies in managing your investments.

Learn to let go.

Act boldly

Entrepreneurs often bristle at the suggestion that taking less risk is the key to success. If I haven't been clear enough yet: remember that low risk certainly doesn't mean no risk.

No risk is a recipe for failure.

Low risk is about taking the right risks and being paid well in exchange for taking them.

Low risk does not suggest that we cower in a corner.

The opposite is true. When we know the odds are on our side, we need to act decisively. Rooting our investment process in a value and quality approach and ignoring the noise from those who are playing a different game allows us to do this with confidence.

The higher stocks go, the more risky they are.

The lower they go, the less risky they are.

Low-risk investing calls for bold action when market prices reflect widespread negativity.

This is the exact time when others' expectations for the future will be low. You need to use the skills you have accumulated over the years to be the maverick, to think independently, and to step up.

The entrepreneur and the investor speak different languages. This is true.

But they also speak the same language—the language of opportunity. Acting boldly when the odds are in your favor, even when everyone else might think you are making a mistake.

You didn't get here by following the crowd. Neither did the world's best investors.

Let go of the fear of missing out and the instinct to chase others.

Act boldly when the odds are stacked in your favor. Take these opportunities to build your empire.

The low-risk road is the narrow, less-traveled path. And more likely to lead to the destination you have in mind.

These are the rules of low-risk investing.

This is the road to success.

JUST THE RULES

_____

Staying rich takes different skills than getting rich.

Let your purpose guide you.

Acknowledge the role of luck and approach wealth preservation with humility.

Be careful with liquidity. Often the wisest thing to do is nothing at all.

Don't invest for entertainment. Let you portfolio bore you.

Approach your investment portfolio with business smarts.

Keeping it simple and understanding your strategy helps you hold on when things get difficult.

Ignore the crowd—most are playing a different game than you are.

Know the difference between investing and speculating. And then invest, don't speculate.

There is no such thing as passive investing. All investing entails making certain choices and accepting certain risks. Only take risks you understand.

NOTES

Introduction

"The end object of..." George J.W. Goodman (writing as Adam Smith), *The Money Game* (Penguin, 1976; 1968).

Chapter 1: Shift Your Perspective

"It would be some relief..." Seneca the Younger, *Letters from a Stoic*, translated by Robin Campbell (Penguin, 1969).

Chapter 2: Focus on Your North Star

"For beyond the satisfaction of..." Arthur Schopenhauer, *The Wisdom of Life* (Project Gutenberg ebook edition, 2004; 1851), gutenberg.org/files/10741/10741-h/10741-h.htm.

"Remember Warren Buffett's sage advice..." Richard I. Kirkland Jr., "Should You Leave It All to the Children?" *Fortune*, September 29, 1986, archive.fortune.com/magazines/fortune/fortune_archive/1986/09/29/68098/index.htm.

Chapter 3: You're Bad at This

"Know the enemy..." Sun Tzu, *The Art of War*, translated by John Minford (Penguin, 2006).

"writes about an experiment..." James O'Shaughnessy, *What Works on Wall Street* (McGraw-Hill, 2011; 1997).

"people consistently consider changes..." Tom Meyvis and Heeyoung Yoon, "Adding Is Favoured over Subtracting in Problem Solving," *Nature*, April 7, 2021, nature.com/articles/d41586-021-00592-0.

"In a 2017 paper…" Diego Liechti, Claudio Loderer, Urs Peyer, and Urs Waelchli, "Luck and Entrepreneurship," Simon Business School working paper no. FR 17-20, February 18, 2017, doi.org/10.2139/ssrn.3028539.

"Lethargy bordering on sloth…" Warren Buffet, letter to Berkshire Hathaway shareholders, Berkshire Hathaway, 1990, berkshire hathaway.com/letters/1990.html.

"that idea led him to make…" Llama Capital, "The Investment Charlie Munger Waited Fifty Years to Make," Trekking with Llama, Substack, February 4, 2021, llamacapital.substack.com/p/the-investment -charlie-munger-waited.

"the famous 1979 Kahneman/Tversky…" Daniel Kahneman and Amos Tversky, "Prospect Theory: An Analysis of Decision under Risk," *Econometrica* 47:2, March 1979, doi.org/10.2307/1914185.

"There is nothing so disturbing…" Charles P. Kindleberger and Robert Z. Aliber, *Manias, Panics, and Crashes: A History of Financial Crises* (Wiley, 2005; 1978).

Chapter 4: Don't Just Do Something, Sit There

"Men who can both be right…" Edwin Lefèvre, *Reminiscences of a Stock Operator* (Wiley Investment Classics, 2006; 1923).

"through the story of Mr. Market…" Benjamin Graham, *The Intelligent Investor: The Definitive Book on Value Investing*, revised edition (Harper Business, 2006; 1949)

"Zuckerberg refused an offer…" Allison Fass, "Peter Thiel Talks About the Day Mark Zuckerberg Turned Down Yahoo's $1 Billion," *Inc.*, March 12, 2013, inc.com/allison-fass/peter-thiel-mark-zuckerberg-luck-day -facebook-turned-down-billion-dollars.html.

"The more frequently you look…" Real Vision Finance, "Grant Williams in Conversation with Anthony Deden," YouTube video, posted July 5, 2018, youtube.com/watch?v=a4_U6bS-cU4.

"elevated cortisol levels…" John Nofsinger, Fernando Patterson, and Corey Shank, "On the Physiology of Investment Biases: The Role of Cortisol and Testosterone," research paper, February 29, 2020, doi.org/10.2139/ssrn.3546687.

Chapter 5: You're Good at This

"Wall Street is the only place…" Linda Grant, "The $4-Billion Regular Guy: Junk Bonds, No. Greenmail, Never. Warren Buffett Invests Money the Old-Fashioned Way," *Los Angeles Times*, April 7, 1991, latimes.com/ archives/la-xpm-1991-04-07-tm-354-story.html.

Chapter 6: Live Slow, Die Old

"People spend all this time…" "Pros: Peter Lynch," *Frontline*, PBS, pbs.org/
wgbh/pages/frontline/shows/betting/pros/lynch.html.

Chapter 7: Your Assets Are Their Income

"Wealthy people tend to have…" Nassim Nicholas Taleb, "Commencement
Address, American University in Beirut," Medium, August 14, 2016,
nntaleb.medium.com/commencement-address-american-university
-in-beirut-2016-a5c6d57984b.

"Important people like to deal…" Mark Graham, "The Commandments
of Business Growth," Entrepreneurs' Organization, January 30, 2012,
blog.eonetwork.org/2012/01/the-commandments-of-business
-growth.

Chapter 8: Challenge the Prestige Investment Pitch

"I know one guy…" Jason Zweig, "A Fireside Chat with Charlie Munger,"
Wall Street Journal, September 12, 2014, wsj.com/articles/BL-MBB
-26843.

Chapter 9: Costs Matter

"To earn the highest returns…" John Bogle, *Common Sense on Mutual Funds*
(Wiley, 2010; 1999).

"Impact of fees on Investment Return graph" Raw data from Morningstar
Direct, via CFA Institute Research Foundation, Monthly Stocks,
Bonds, Bills, Inflation (SBBI) Dataset, provided by email.

"Smith played out a 'what-if'…" Terry Smith, *Investing for Growth: How to
Make Money by Only Buying the Best Companies in the World* (Harriman
House, 2020).

Chapter 10: You Are Not an Institution

"Simplicity has been difficult…" Nassim Nicholas Taleb, *Antifragile: Things
That Gain from Disorder* (Random House, 2012).

"In a 2014 paper…" Tim Jenkinson, Howard Jones, and Jose
Vicente Martinez, "Picking Winners? Investment Consultants'
Recommendations of Fund Managers," *Journal of Finance* 71:5,
October 2016, 2333-2369, doi.org/10.1111/jofi.12289.

"Consultants express conventional…" David F. Swensen, *Pioneering
Portfolio Management* (Simon and Schuster, 2000).

"Ennis concludes that large…" Richard Ennis, "Failure of the Endowment
Model," draft paper, November 26, 2020, richardmennis.com/blog/
failure-of-the-standard-model-of-institutional-investment.

Chapter 11: The Volatility You Can't See Is Still There

"'How did you go bankrupt?'..." Ernest Hemingway, *The Sun Also Rises* (Scribner, 2006; 1926).

"*Since 2008, studies have demonstrated...*" Sebastien Canderle, "Myths of Private Equity Performance: Part III," CFA Institute, December 16, 2020, blogs.cfainstitute.org/investor/2020/12/16/myths-of-private-equity-performance-part-iii.

"*hedge fund indices are mostly...*" Johann Colloredo-Mansfeld and Dan Rasmussen, "What's the Point of Hedge Funds?" Verdad Weekly Research newsletter, August 2, 2021, mailchi.mp/verdadcap/whats-the-point-of-hedge-funds.

"*Guggenheim investment company estimates...*" Guggenheim, "Asset Class Correlation Map," guggenheiminvestments.com/mutual-funds/resources/interactive-tools/asset-class-correlation-map.

"*EnCap's valuation team had woefully...*" Jamie Powell, "Private Equity and the Mark-to-Market Myth," *Financial Times*, January 28, 2020, ft.com/content/a09f0885-f15a-4ad3-b4ae-3bc9f2bc5430; and Selin Bucak, "Private Equity Comes under Pressure for More Transparency on Marking of Assets," *Private Equity News*, February 3, 2020, penews.com/articles/what-is-your-portfolio-really-worth-20200203.

"*Asness asks, 'What if investors...'*" Cliff Asness, "The Illiquidity Discount?" AQR, December 19, 2019, aqr.com/Insights/Perspectives/the-illiquidity-discount.

"*once he stopped trying to time...*" David Chambers, Elroy Dimson, and Justin Foo, "Keynes the Stock Market Investor: A Quantitative Analysis," *Journal of Financial and Quantitative Analysis* 50:4, August 2015, doi.org/10.2139/ssrn.2023011.

"*One must not allow...*" Justyn Walsh, *Keynes and the Market: How the World's Greatest Economist Overturned Conventional Wisdom and Made a Fortune on the Stock Market* (John Wiley & Sons, 2008).

Chapter 12: The Volatility You Can See Is Lying to You

"*I can calculate the motions...*" Sir Isaac Newton, as quoted by Shahid Mahmood, "The Motion of Heavenly Bodies," *Huffpost*, November 5, 2012, huffpost.com/entry/the-motion-of-heavenly-bo_b_1853969.

"*comments on the YouTube clip...*" Highlight Hell, "Marion Barber: The Greatest 2 Yard Run Ever (Patriots vs. Cowboys 2007)," YouTube video, posted July 25, 2020, youtube.com/watch?v=bzUTn-PEPYU.

"quoted a hedge fund manager who…" David Wells, "Amazon Shares Touch 3-Year Low on Profit Skepticism," *Bloomberg*, September 6, 2011, blinks.bloomberg.com/news/stories/GJ9A910D9L35.

"just another middleman…" Jacqueline Doherty, "Amazon.bomb," *Barron's*, May 31, 1999, barrons.com/articles/SB9279322627532 84707.

"I don't pay attention…" The Grant Williams Podcast, "The End Game Episode 11: Jim Rogers," November 14, 2020, grant-williams.com/podcast/the-end-game-ep-11-jim-rogers.

"Gray theorized an omnipotent…" Wesley Gray, "Even God Would Get Fired as an Active Investor," Alpha Architect, February 2, 2016, alphaarchitect.com/2016/02/02/even-god-would-get-fired-as-an-active-investor.

Chapter 13: Keep It Simple, Keep It Liquid

"Simplicity is the…" Widely attributed to Leonardo da Vinci, but there is no evidence that he ever actually said it. The saying was a favorite of Steve Jobs and was used on the cover of the brochure introducing the Apple II computer in 1978.

"Venture capital has become…" Charles Duhigg, "How Venture Capitalists Are Deforming Capitalism," *New Yorker*, November 23, 2020, newyorker.com/magazine/2020/11/30/how-venture-capitalists-are-deforming-capitalism.

"Usually 90 percent…" John Authers, "Authers Notes: Charles D. Ellis on 'Winning the Loser's Game,'" *Bloomberg*, October 18, 2021, bloomberg.com/opinion/articles/2021-10-18/authers-notes-charles-d-ellis-on-winning-the-loser-s-game.

"he was unable to repay $6 million…" Lester Munson, "Bad Advice, Bad Decisions: The Loss of Michael Vick's Fortune," ESPN, August 15, 2008, espn.com/nfl/columns/story?columnist=munson_lester&id=3537577.

"he told the story of an unnamed athlete…" via Making Sense with Ed Butowsky, "How and Why Professional Athletes Go Broke: Ed Butowsky," YouTube video, posted December 7, 2012, youtube.com/watch?v=hqJqqbpcc4E.

"Take Mark Rothko…" Jack Hough, "Putting Money in the Banksy: How Investing in Shares of Art Compares with Stocks," *Barron's*, November 20, 2020, barrons.com/articles/investing-in-art-looks-profitable-on-paperbut-looks-can-be-deceiving-51605914355.

Chapter 14: Play Your Own Game

"Investment is most intelligent…" Benjamin Graham, *The Intelligent Investor*.

Chapter 15: The Market Is Not Your Friend

"The main purpose of…" Bernard Baruch is commonly credited with this quote, but the exact source is uncertain. See Barry Popik, BarryPopik .com, October 18, 2008 blog entry, barrypopik.com/index.php/ new_york_city/entry/the_main_purpose_of_the_stock_market_is_to_ make_fools_of_as_many_men_as_pos.

Chapter 16: Get Paid to Take Risk

"When you boil it all…" Howard Marks, *The Most Important Thing* (Columbia Business School Publishing, 2011).

"I just couldn't stand it…" Trung Phan, "Stanley Druckenmiller: 'The Greatest Investors Make Large Concentrated Bets Where They Have a Lot of Conviction,'" *The Hustle*, May 26, 2021, thehustle.co/ stanley-druckenmiller-q-and-a-trung-phanin.

"I bought $6 billion…" Tyler Durden, "Stan Druckenmiller Recounts His $3 Billion 'Lesson' from the Tech Bubble," *Zero Hedge*, September 3, 2020, zerohedge.com/political/stan-druckenmiller-recounts-his -3-billion-lesson-tech-bubble.

"Who cares? All I know…" Jason Zweig, "Did You Beat the Market"? *Money*, January 2000, available at jasonzweig.com/from-the-archives-did -you-beat-the-market.

Chapter 17: Understand Why Low Risk Rules

"To enjoy a reasonable chance…" Benjamin Graham, *The Intelligent Investor*.

"high-beta assets tend to have…" Michael C. Jensen, Fischer Black, and Myron Scholes, "The Capital Asset Pricing Model: Some Empirical Tests," *Studies in the Theory of Capital Markets*, 1972, papers.ssrn .com/sol3/papers.cfm?abstract_id=908569.

"after observing the performance…" Robert A. Haugen and A. James Heins, "On the Evidence Supporting the Existence of Risk Premiums in the Capital Market," research paper, December 1, 1972, doi.org/10.2139/ ssrn.1783797.

"underestimate the average returns…" Eugene F. Fama and Kenneth R. French, "The Cross-Section of Expected Stock Returns," *The Journal of Finance* 47:2, June 1992, doi.org/10.2307/2329112.

"low-volatility and low-beta portfolios..." Malcolm P. Baker, Brendan
Bradley, and Jeffrey Wurgler, "Benchmarks as Limits to Arbitrage:
Understanding the Low Volatility Anomaly," NYU working paper
No. 2451/29593, March 2010, ssrn.com/abstract=1585031.

"compelling evidence for the anomaly..." Nardin L. Baker and Robert
A. Haugen, "Low Risk Stocks Outperform Within All Observable
Markets of the World," research paper, April 27, 2012, doi.org/
10.2139/ssrn.2055431.

"twenty international equity markets..." Andrea Frazzini and Lasse Heje
Pedersen, "Betting Against Beta," *Journal of Financial Economics*
111:1, January 2014, doi.org/10.1016/j.jfineco.2013.10.005.

"a dollar invested in the lowest-risk portfolio..." Malcolm P. Baker,
Brendan Bradley, and Ryan Taliaferro, "The Low Risk Anomaly:
A Decomposition into Micro and Macro Effects," *Financial Analysts
Journal*, September 13, 2013, doi.org/10.2139/ssrn.2210003.

"they authored two papers..." David Blitz and Pim van Vliet, "The Volatility
Effect: Lower Risk Without Lower Return," *Journal of Portfolio
Management*, Fall 2007, papers.ssrn.com/sol3/papers.cfm?abstract_
id=980865; and, with Guido Baltussen, "The Volatility Effect
Revisited," *Journal of Portfolio Management* 46:2, October 2019,
doi.org/10.3905/jpm.2019.1.114.

"the deck is stacked against high volatility..." Robert Novy-Marx,
"Understanding Defensive Equity," NBER working paper no. w20591,
October 2014, ssrn.com/abstract=2513151.

"the anomaly is much more about..." Larry E. Swedroe and Andrew L.
Berkin, *Your Complete Guide to Factor-Based Investing* (Bam Alliance
Press, 2016).

"bettors prefer long-shot horses..." R.M. Griffith, "Odds Adjustments by
American Horse-Race Bettors," *American Journal of Psychology*, April
1, 1949, doi.org/10.2307/1418469.

"The biggest risk is not..." Mellody Hobson, *Total Return* newsletter, April
2007, available at arielinvestments.com/images/stories/PDF/04.07
%20hobson.pdf (pdf download).

Chapter 18: Invest, Don't Speculate

"In the short run..." This has been widely quoted in various versions,
but the original source is uncertain. This popularized form is thought
to have originated with Warren Buffett, quoting from a conversation
with Graham. See: quoteinvestigator.com/2020/01/09/market.

"Prospect theory tells us…" Daniel Kahneman and Amos Tversky,
"Prospect Theory: An Analysis of Decision Under Risk," *Econometrica*
47:2, March 1979, doi.org/10.2307/1914185.

Chapter 19: Honor Your Investment Edge

"The stock market is…" As quoted by John Reese in "Winning in the
Market with the Patience of the Wright Brothers and Warren Buffett,"
Forbes, January 30, 2018, forbes.com/sites/investor/2018/01/30/
winning-in-the-market-with-the-patience-of-the-wright-brothers
-and-warren-buffett.

Chapter 20: Embrace Boredom

"If investing is entertaining…" This has been widely quoted; the original
source is uncertain. See: "Billionaire George Soros Pulls the Trigger
on These 3 Stocks," August 17, 2021, *Yahoo Finance*, finance.yahoo
.com/news/billionaire-george-soros-pulls-trigger-134555270.html.

"researchers confirmed a 1996 analysis…" Pedro Bordalo, Nicola
Gennaioli, Rafael La Porta, and Andrei Shleifer, "Diagnostic
Expectations and Stock Returns," *Journal of Finance* 74:6, July 6,
2019, doi.org/10.1111/jofi.12833.

"He takes the top 1,000 US companies…" Steven Romick, "History
Shows That High Earnings Growth Is Unsustainable," The Aquirer's
Multiple, September 21, 2021, acquirersmultiple.com/2021/09/
steven-romick-history-shows-that-high-earnings-growth-is
-unsustainable.

"specialized ETFs that track…" Itzhak Ben-David, Francesco Franzoni,
Byungwook Kim, and Rabih Moussawi, "Competition for Attention
in the ETF Space," Fisher College of Business working paper no.
2021-03-001, January 14, 2021, doi.org/10.2139/ssrn.3765063.

Chapter 21: Conviction Is the Key

"If you would not have…" Seneca the Younger, *The Complete Works of Seneca the
Younger*, translation by Richard Mott Gunmere (Delphi Classics, 2014).

"in 2018 they noted that the average…" RBC Global Asset Management,
"The Influence of Investor Behaviour," May 2018, ca.rbcwealth
management.com/documents/48092/48112/influence-of-investor
-behavior.pdf/00dadc04-e19b-407d-a32a-124edf1ad0f1.

"In 2007 alone, the fund was up…" Eleanor Laise, "Best Stock Fund of the
Decade: CGM Focus," *Wall Street Journal*, December 31, 2009, wsj
.com/articles/SB10001424052748704876804574628561609012
716.

Chapter 22: Take Responsibility

"And the high priests of modern..." Benoit Mandelbrot, *The (Mis)Behavior of Markets*, annotated edition (Basic Books, 2006; 2004).

"about $13.5 trillion benchmarked to the index..." S&P Global, S&P 500 overview, spglobal.com/spdji/en/indices/equity/sp-500/#overview.

"only sixty of the original 500..." Matthew De Silva, "The Art and Science of Stewarding the S&P 500," *Yahoo Finance*, September 25, 2019, finance.yahoo.com/news/art-science-stewarding-p-500-100055 369.html.

"with the average tenure declining..." Scott D. Anthony, S. Patrick Viguerie, Evan I. Schwartz, and John Van Landeghem, "2018 Corporate Longevity Forecast: Creative Destruction Is Accelerating," Innosight executive briefing, February 2018, innosight.com/wp-content/ uploads/2017/11/Innosight-Corporate-Longevity-2018.pdf (pdf download).

"there are now more indices than..." Bloomberg, "There Are Now More Indices Than Stocks," May 12, 2017, bloomberg.com/news/articles/ 2017-05-12/there-are-now-more-indexes-than-stocks.

"the S&P 500 is dominated by..." Edward Yardeni, "Industry Indicators: FANGS," Yardeni Research, accessed September 21, 2021, yardeni .com/pub/yardenifangoverview.pdf (pdf download).

"the market was dominated by the 'Nifty Fifty'..." Ben Carlson, "The Nifty Fifty and the Old Normal," *A Wealth of Common Sense*, July 2, 2020, awealthofcommonsense.com/2020/07/the-nifty-fifty-and-the -old-normal.

Chapter 23: Know What You Own

"If you are going to be..." Attributed to Michael J. Burry in Michael Lewis, *The Big Short: Inside the Doomsday Machine* (W.W. Norton, 2010).

Chapter 24: It's Art, Not Science

"Investing in stocks is..." Peter Lynch, *One Up on Wall Street*, second edition (Simon & Schuster, 2000; 1989).

Conclusion: Let Go and Act Boldly

"The secret is to..." Attributed to Niki Lauda in Clive James, "Winning Slowly," *The Monthly*, April 2006, themonthly.com.au/nation -reviewed-clive-james-winning-slowly—194.

INDEX

Page references to figures are in *italic*.

ABOUT THE AUTHOR

GEOFF SAAB is a wealth manager who has held various positions in tax, estate planning, and insurance, and now serves clients as a portfolio manager within an investment counsel firm. He spent over a decade working in a single-family office, advocating directly on behalf of his clients. With his unique experience of working as both a wealth management industry insider and outsider, he has gained a deep understanding of how the industry works (and doesn't work) for clients.

BUILD YOUR EMPIRE

———————

Thanks for spending some time with *Low Risk Rules*. I hope it helps you clarify your goals, simplify your portfolio, and focus on what matters.

If you're an investor and this book resonates with you, let's stay in touch.

If you're an advisor or portfolio manager and would like to share the gospel of low-risk investing with your clients and prospects, please contact me for bulk order discounts and more. I'd be happy to help in any way I can!

You can find me here: **geoffsaab.com**

I'm looking forward to hearing from you!

www.ingramcontent.com/pod-product-compliance
Lightning Source LLC
Chambersburg PA
CBHW030457210326
41597CB00013B/700